**Jake Pi**

# From Working to Surfing

**Everything you need to know about a working holiday in**

# Australia

*From Working to Surfing*
*Everything you need to know about*
*Australia*



*Published by Jake Pitts Publishing*

*Originally published in the United Kingdom by Jake Pitts*

*This book is a work of non fiction based on the experiences, recollections and knowledge of the authors travels of Australia.*

*The information is subject to change over time and certain parts of the book may become uncertain, due to changes made by any organisation or person that is mentioned in the book.*

*The Author has taken all the photos personally except a few which were taken by other travellers which the author knows personally except the flag of Australia image.*

*Introduction*

Chapter 1- What the Books about
Chapter 2- Facts on Australia
Chapter 3- Weather
Chapter 4- Arriving in Oz

*Necessities*

Chapter 5- Banking and ATM
Chapter 6- Phone Providers
Chapter 7- Medicare and Health
Chapter 8- Travel Insurance
Chapter 9- Where to Live
Chapter 10- Tax File Number (TFN)
Chapter 11- Getting a Job
Chapter 12-Tax Back and Superannuation

*Visas and Farm Work*

Chapter 13- Getting a Visa
Chapter 14- Farm Work
Chapter 15- Getting a Second Year Visa
Chapter 16- Living Permanently in Australia

*Hostels and Intro Packages*

Chapter 17- Hostel Life
Chapter 18- Meeting New People
Chapter 19- Security/Travel Safety
Chapter 20- Intro Packages Advantages and Disadvantages

*Costs and Shopping*

Chapter 21- Average Costs Breakdown
Chapter 22- Shopping
Chapter 23- Where to Party? and Drinking
Chapter 24- Budgeting Your Money

*Transportation*

Chapter 25- Local/Public Transport

Chapter 26- Buses Around Australia
Chapter 27- Trains Around Australia
Chapter 28- Domestic Flying in Australia
Chapter 29- Buying a Car/Van
Chapter 30- Renting a Car/Van
Chapter 31- Hitch-Hiking

*Places to Go*

Chapter 32- What to do in Sydney
Chapter 33- What to do in Melbourne
Chapter 34- Travelling the East Coast
Chapter 35- Travelling the West Coast
Chapter 36- Uluru/The Red Centre
Chapter 37- Other Places Worth Stopping

*Before you Go*

Chapter 38- My Mistakes
Chapter 39- Before you go Check-list
Chapter 40- What to Pack
Chapter 41- Long Haul Flying
Chapter 42- Leaving Home
Chapter 43- Returning Home

# Introduction

## Chapter 1-What the Books about

Welcome to the Ultimate Guide to your Working Holiday in Australia. I hope your excited because your about to embark on one of the biggest adventures of your life and everything you could want to know is in this book from setting up a bank account, best places to visit, good night life spots and necessities like your TFN, finding a job and getting an Apartment. If this all sounds like a lot to deal with and like it could be stressful.. no worries as everything you need to know is right at hand and just a page turn away.

Well a little bit about me the guy that's giving you all this information.. I had always wanted to travel after high school as I wanted to get out into the world, meet new people, visit new places and gain life experience and lessons that you could never learn in a classroom. So after a little bit of research I decided to pick Australia and what a fantastic choice it turned out to be the land of Golden Beaches, Green Forests and incredible people. I left for Down Under when I was 19 and this was my first solo trip, literally couldn't get much further away from home, and that's what this book is here to help you with as this is a guide from someone that's been there themselves, done it, made the mistakes and here to give you advice on what to do and what you probably shouldn't do. If you've brought this book and are still a little unsure as to whether you want to go or not. Whether your 18 and have just finished school or your 30 and just want to see what working and travelling in another country is like, just do it if you've got a little bit of money saved up honestly take the leap, it was definitely one of the best things I did and taught me invaluable lessons which have helped me and I'm sure will continue to help me incredible amounts. As well as that it's the lifelong friends you meet and contacts you make that will continue to serve you long into the future and of course the main reason the majority of us go travelling, the chance to see new places and indulge yourself into a complete new culture and community.

## Chapter 2-Facts On Australia

Capital - Canberra ... Surprisingly not Sydney as a lot of people seem to think.
Largest City - Sydney
Main Cities - Sydney, Melbourne, Perth, Brisbane, Adelaide, Hobart and Darwin
National Language - English
Flag:

Area - 2,969,907 sq miles or 7,692,024 sq km

Highest Mainland Point - Mount Kosciuszko at 2,228 meters

Population – 23,867,800 (2015 estimate)

GDP (Measure of size of the economy) - $1. 137 trillion

Currency - Australian Dollar (AUD)

Time Zone - Various (UTC +8 to +10.5)

Drivers on the - Left

Calling Code - +61

Minimum Wage - The national minimum wage is $17.29 per hour or $656.90 per 38 hour working week (Before Tax).

Australia is the worlds sixth largest country by area and is made up of six states; Western Australia, Queensland, South Australia, New South Wales, Victoria and the Northern Territory. Australia's culturally diverse society includes its Indigenous people who arrived more than 40,000 years ago and people have continually been drawn to live in Australia from all over the world now hosting to people from over 140 countries.

## Chapter 3-Weather

Australia is a very big Country so the weather is very diverse depending on where you are. For example living up in north Queensland and Darwin areas it's hot all year round and perfect if you need a tan whereas down south like Tasmania and Melbourne in the winters it gets very cold even sometimes as low as minus temperatures. Australia is also one of the driest continents in the world experiencing less than 600ml of rainfall a year. Also like all of the countries in the southern hemisphere of the world, Australia's Seasons are opposite to the northern Hemisphere so opposite to all of Europe. December to February is summer, March to May is autumn, June to August is winter and September to November is spring. So basically in the UK's winter it's warm and in the UK's summer it's cold.

Average Weather Per Capital Cities:

| Adelaide: | Min | Max |
|---|---|---|
| Summer (Dec-Feb)- | 16 | 29 |
| Autumn (Mar-May)- | 13 | 23 |
| Winter (Jun-Aug)- | 7 | 15 |
| Spring (Sep-Nov)- | 11 | 22 |

| Brisbane: | Min | Max |
|---|---|---|
| Summer (Dec-Feb)- | 21 | 29 |
| Autumn (Mar-May)- | 17 | 27 |
| Winter (Jun-Aug)- | 10 | 21 |
| Spring (Sep-Nov)- | 16 | 26 |

| Darwin (Northern Territory): | Min | Max |
| --- | --- | --- |
| Summer (Dec-Feb)- | 25 | 32 |
| Autumn (Mar-May)- | 24 | 33 |
| Winter (Jun-Aug)- | 19 | 30 |
| Spring (Sep-Nov)- | 25 | 33 |

| Hobart (Tasmania): | Min | Max |
| --- | --- | --- |
| Summer (Dec-Feb)- | 12 | 21 |
| Autumn (Mar-May)- | 9 | 17 |
| Winter (Jun-Aug)- | 5 | 12 |
| Spring (Sep-Nov)- | 8 | 17 |

| Melbourne (Victoria): | Min | Max |
| --- | --- | --- |
| Summer (Dec-Feb)- | 18 | 26 |
| Autumn (Mar-May)- | 8 | 24 |
| Winter (Jun-Aug)- | 6 | 15 |
| Spring (Sep-Nov)- | 8 | 22 |

| Perth (Western Australia): | Min | Max |
| --- | --- | --- |
| Summer (Dec-Feb)- | 18 | 30 |
| Autumn (Mar-May)- | 14 | 25 |
| Winter (Jun-Aug)- | 9 | 18 |
| Spring (Sep-Nov)- | 12 | 22 |

| Sydney (New South Wales): | Min | Max |
| --- | --- | --- |
| Summer (Dec-Feb)- | 19 | 29 |
| Autumn (Mar-May)- | 15 | 22 |
| Winter (Jun-Aug)- | 8 | 16 |
| Spring (Sep-Nov)- | 13 | 22 |

| Alice Springs (Central Australia): | Min | Max |
|---|---|---|
| Summer (Dec-Feb)- | 21 | 36 |
| Autumn (Mar-May)- | 13 | 28 |
| Winter (Jun-Aug)- | 19 | 30 |
| Spring (Sep-Nov)- | 25 | 33 |

So now you know what temperatures certain places are at specific times of the year, but where would I recommend being at what time of the year. Well I spent my summer months in Sydney working and what an incredible summer it was, festivals, beaches, surfing and BBQs, it was just what you picture when you think of a summer abroad and the weather on the weekends often getting into the low thirty's. Plus the obvious bonus of being in Sydney during the summer is getting to spend Christmas on the beach with some cold beers, definitely a Christmas you wont forget. Not forgetting new years eve in Sydney, this is always a huge event starting off with Sydney's famous fireworks and then hitting one of the huge after parties... what better way to spend NYE, or if you're on a bigger budget I would definitely recommend a NYE party harbour cruise. I would also recommend Melbourne and Perth for the summer months Melbourne is not so big on beaches though it does have a few and will probably be a little cooler, but will still have those warm days and if your into your art, little cafés and alleyways I'd probably check out Melbourne, it reminded me of a European city. Perth on the west coast again really warm in the summer months and has amazing beaches some of the best surf in Australia can be found a few hours south of Perth too if you want to catch a bus. The only problem with me for Perth is that it's a little quite and you could soon get bored of it this is from my own personal experience, and a lot of travellers that did live in Perth for long periods said you could soon get bored as there's not a huge scene for travellers, but definitely worth a visit during the summer for a week or so as it's still a beautiful area of Australia.

I would recommend doing your farm work in Autumn or Spring I did some of mine in the summer in Queensland and it was scorching hot, having to wear long clothing and walking down a field picking vegetables/fruit in near 40c is not nice. Whereas in spring and autumn it will be a lot cooler still a little warm but not as warm as that scorching summer heat, and I wouldn't do it in the winter for obvious reasons as it can get really cold. Yes even in Australia and that's not really what you want when your stuck on a farm with limited supplies of everything including heat. One of the most popular things to do in Australia is the East Coast. I'm sure you've head of it if your planning on doing a working holiday. Working your way from Sydney to Cairns or Cairns to Sydney. I would definitely do it from Sydney to Cairns rather than the other way around as this way it's only going to get warmer rather than colder. The time of year for this doesn't matter too much I wouldn't do it in winter as it would be very cold even a fair way up the coast and would ruin a lot of the stuff to do like the beaches and surfing, obviously the summer sounds perfect but it is a little more expensive so once again if you have a large budget do it in the summer. But in my opinion I would recommend doing it in the spring or autumn this way you are leaving the cold of the cities like Melbourne or Sydney and heading up north to warmer climates. Doing it this way you get the hot summer in the city and then as its turning cold you can move up the coast as its only going to get warmer the further up you travel, it will also be a little cheaper as it wont be in the heat of summer but you'll still get the warmth of spring and autumn.

## Chapter 4-Arriving in Oz

So upon arriving in Australia there are a few main things you are going to want to get sorted first, of course everybody wants to get out exploring straight away and get seeing the sights but trust me there's plenty of time for that later and there is probably a few things that you need to sort out too.

When first arriving in whichever city at the airport make sure you have the address and name of the hostel your staying at and I would definitely recommend having somewhere pre booked for at least the first 3 nights it just saves you worrying about having to find somewhere to stay and if you cant find a room especially if your tired after a long haul flight you don't want to be trekking around an unknown city looking for a bed. So once you arrive at the airport, have collected your baggage, gone through customs etc. You're going to want to get to your hostel and get checked in. I would recommend getting a train or shuttle from the airports as it's going to be a lot cheaper than getting a taxi especially if your by yourself and will not be that much slower. Sydney airport you can get the train into the city for $10 it's super easy literally just follow the signs. And for any other major airports you can book a shuttle to the city just outside the airport there will be taxi's maybe buses and shuttles just walk up to the shuttle desk and say you want to go to the city it shouldn't cost you more than $15 and will get you there pretty quick some hostels even offer a free shuttle from the airport, so make sure you check that out when your booking your hostel as it'll just drop you off right outside your hostel which is perfect when just arriving and your tired.

So once you've arrived at your hostel and your all checked in and into your room, make sure you introduce yourself to everyone in your room tell them your name spend a bit of time getting to know them, find out how long there staying what there doing that night and ask if you can join them later on, straight away you've got some people you can chill with for a bit and also get to learn a bit about the city and what they've been up to. For the first day I would just catch up on sleep get to know the area a bit and relax depending on how your feeling or you could just go and sort your basic stuff out straight away. Definitely go and get some food and put it in the fridge it's much cheaper than eating out and you'll get to meet lots more people in the kitchen when your cooking and eating. After that the main things you're going to want to get sorted out is your bank card, a mobile phone Sim and phone plan and maybe a job and an apartment depending on what your plans are but I'll explain more about all that stuff in Chapter 2. After I'd sorted out these few things I would probably just enjoy my first week exploring the city, meeting new people and doing all the touristy things you planned to do before you left. Then in the second week start looking for a job if you want to work first and an apartment or maybe you want to stay and live in a hostel for a while, or start planning your travels and people to go with. Dependent on what you want to do after your first week or what your plans are will depend on what you want to do next but that's just a rough idea of what to do when first arriving in Oz.

I would also recommend getting your regional farm work done early if you can. If you want to get your second year visa in Australia definitely try to get it done as soon as possible as it will save you a lot of stress later on. I met a lot of people on the farms who left it until the last minute and it caused a lot of stress and problems, sometimes farms run out of work or you may get fired etc. This is very bad if you don't have many days to spare before you have to leave the country and you may run out of time and not be able to get your second year visa so definitely get that done sooner rather than later. Also dependent on your money situation if you are looking for a job as soon as you get to Australia I would recommend going to Sydney as jobs are plentiful here and very easy to get, ranging from call centres to bar work there's lots of opportunity, it's got a really good backpacker scene too so is relatively cheap to live. Melbourne also offers good job opportunities and has similar prices to Sydney, so dependent on what you want, that should decide where you should head to. Places like Perth and Cairns are a little bit more expensive and there are no where near as many jobs for backpackers, they are available and you can get them, just it may take a little longer and a lot more searching. I would recommend working before travelling though as this gives you more of a chance to plan where you want to go, save some money for your travels, and meet some like minded travellers to go with, as trust me plans often change when travelling you may plan to do one thing but that can all soon change when someone gives you another idea or travel proposal.

# Necessities

## Chapter 5-Banking and ATM

Unfortunately, this part of the book helps you with all the boring stuff, the stuff that everyone has to do especially if you want to work in Australia, but it's the essential stuff that without doing you wouldn't be able to do all the fun stuff. So to start banking. There's a lot of choices with banking the same as in any other country there's loads of choices of accounts and branches. One thing I would highly recommend is setting up and Australian bank account before you even leave your own country. This is really simple to do and can be done online in as little as 5 minutes. You just go onto the bank of your choices website and can set up the bank account often just filling in a couple of forms, you can even do this as far as up to 12 months before you head to Australia. Then you can transfer money into it when you're ready. I would definitely recommend doing this as then the money is in your Australian bank account when you arrive, doing this saves you a lot of money in transfer fees or getting travellers cheques, and also saves you carrying cash and the chance of losing it. The only cost you will pay will be from your home account for transferring it and this was £20 for me and a sometimes you might be charged some from the receiver, but it wont be a lot and you can always email them to check.

When transferring your money from your home bank account they will ask you how much you want to transfer and will give you a conversion rate, telling you how much in Australian dollars will be in your bank account. You can then check this online to make sure its there, it can take up to 5 working days maybe more dependent on your bank. Upon arrival in Australia, you just go to the Branch with your passport and they will set it all up for you, you can then collect your cards, they will even help you with online banking and getting an App for your phone which I used all the time, it's so useful and incredibly easy to use.

The Main Banks and Options:
So there are three main banks which I would choose from if your wanting a bank account in Australia. There are others but the reason I picked these three are they are the main banks and most widely used, they also have a lot of cash points all over the country which is very useful for obvious reasons. I myself used Commonwealth Bank and found them to be very helpful and ATM's readily available.

Commonwealth Bank:

- The Bank Account is an everyday account Smart Access.

- There is a $0 ATM withdrawal fee.
- $0 monthly account fees – $4 monthly account fee will be waived if you deposit at least $2,000 per month (or $1000 if you're aged 21 to 24).
- You can access your money anywhere as MasterCard is accepted at over 35 million locations worldwide.
- They have Tap and Pay so you can just tap your card to pay for items.
- Mobile App Banking, which all you need is your secure 4 digit pin to access your accounts from any mobile device.
- Make International money transfers.
- Over 4000 ATM's and 1000 branches in Australia.
- You can apply online in under 10 minutes.
- Withdraw money from an ATM without a card, using Cardless Cash in the Comm-bank app which is incredibly useful if you lose your card and need money while waiting for a new one.
- You also get a few account options with this Card such as a Savings account.

Westpac Bank:

- You get an everyday banking account and a savings account when setting up the bank online.
- $0 monthly service fee for the first 12 months for new migrant and ex-pat customers (other fees apply).
- No withdrawal fee at over 3,000 Westpac, St. George, Bank of Melbourne and BankSA ATM's in Australia.
- Online, Mobile and Tablet banking offering a range of enhanced features to help you bank on the go.
- Has Tap and Pay so you can just tap your card to pay for items without inputting your pin.
- Also offers Cardless cash without a debit card it sends you a code through

text or you can call them which is great if you lose your card.

- No Australian address needed to apply from abroad and it takes as little as 5 minutes.
- Over 3000 ATM's in Australia.

NAB:

- No monthly account fees, ever, no matter how you bank. No minimum deposits.
- Apply online it takes as little as 5 minutes.
- NAB visa debit card with payWave at no extra cost, so you can shop wherever Visa is accepted without entering your pin for amounts up to $100.
- Unlimited access to your money through NAB internet banking or NAB telephone banking, in any branch, through their ATM network (including rediATM's), using EFTPOS, or through an optional cheque book.
- They don't directly charge you for using other ATM's but the owners of other ATM's might directly charge you. If they do, you'll see a message and you'll have the option to quit before you're charged.
- Over 3,400 NAB ATM's in Australia.

## Chapter 6-Phone Providers

So another one of the essential things that you are going to need when getting to Australia is an Australian sim card and telephone number. Your going to need this to be able to call up about jobs, apartment viewings, buying a car and all the other things like when you meet someone new and want to contact them. Once again there are a lot of options in regards to sim card providers and the deals they offer but I will run through the main ones and there benefits. Most of you will bring a phone from home which if you do, make sure its UNLOCKED or else you'll have to pay to get it unlocked which could end up costing you a lot and wasting a lot of your time. If your planning on buying a phone when you get to Australia, then you can pick up a cheap phone which allows facebook, apps, twitter, calls, messages all the basics for about $80. You could also get a contract but I would recommended just getting a PAYG deal as you never know what your going to be doing or when your going to be leaving the country so could end up wasting a lot of money. Whereas if you get a PAYG deal you just top up so much each month and it gives certain amounts of data, calls and messages.

The Main Options:
These are the just the main providers and the options of PAYG deals they have in Australia which is what I would recommended as it will end up saving you a lot of money and you can then control your selections month by month depending on what you want and if your situation changes. All these plans and deals are subject to change. But this is a rough idea and information on the providers.

Optus:
Optus has a range of prepaid monthly deals ranging from $30 a month to $60 a month you simply top up which you can do in most stores, just ask for an optus recharge voucher and then your deal will last for 30 days more or you can top up online. Also with optus you can roll over your data of up to 10GB so if you have any left it carries onto the next month.

- $30 Recharge- Unlimited texts, Unlimited Calls, 1.5GB of Data and $5 extra credit for international calls, roaming and premium services.
- $45 Recharge- Unlimited texts, Unlimited Calls, 3.5GB of Data and $10 extra credit for international calls, roaming and premium services.
- $60 Recharge- Unlimited texts, Unlimited Calls, 6GB of Data and $15 extra credit for international calls, roaming and premium services.

They also offer a prepaid daily sim which charges you for every day you use your mobile, so if your not going to be using your phone everyday say maybe your doing your farm work and don't want to pay $30 if your not using it everyday this is probably a better option.

- $1 a day- Up to 30 minutes calls, unlimited texts and 40MB of data.
- $1.50 a day- Unlimited calls, unlimited texts and 80MB of data.

Also for every extra 50MB of data you use it will cost you an extra 50c, and the day ends at 11.59PM local time.

Vodafone:

Vodafone also has a range of PAYG sim deals but they call them combo packs which when you top up gives you 28 days of whatever is offered in the deal they range from $30-$50. Once again to top up you can do it online or go into most stores and just ask for a Vodafone top up voucher for the amount you want.

- $30 Recharge- $30 of combo credit, unlimited national calls and texts and 1.5GB of data.
- $40 Recharge- $40 of combo credit, unlimited national calls and texts and 3GB of data, 90 minutes of calls from Oz to selected countries.
- $50 Recharge- $50 of combo credit, unlimited national calls and texts and 4GB of data, 90 minutes of calls from Oz to selected countries.

Vodafone also offers a Basic sim which is just where you top up and use it as you use the credit. It costs $1 and then you just top up as and when you need it. Also with Vodafone you can get Add Ons which if you need to add on more data etc. You can do so.

Data Add Ons:

- 2GB = $3, 1 day expiry

- 2GB = $7, 7 day expiry
- 500MB = $5, 28 day expiry
- 1GB =  $10, 28 day expiry
- 2 GB = $15, 28 day expiry

Telstra:

Telstra also offers a range of prepaid sim packages similar to Vodafone and optus, they range from $30-$50. All of the data and credit rolls over onto your next recharge which is very useful and it lasts for 28 days. Same as the others to recharge you can either do this online or just go into a store and ask for a recharge voucher for the amount required.

- $30 recharge- 1.3GB data, unlimited calls to Telstra mobiles, unlimited texts, $250 call credit to standard local numbers and international.
- $40 recharge- 3GB data, unlimited calls to Telstra mobiles, unlimited texts, $750 call credit to standard local numbers and international.
- $50 recharge- 4GB data, unlimited calls to Telstra mobiles, unlimited texts, $1500 call credit to standard local numbers and international.

Telstra also offers a range of other products like, sim deals that last a longer time and flat rate top ups and they also offer bonus top ups if you need extra data and calls.

All of these phone sim cards arrive to you within 5 working days or you can go into a store and pick one up, they will even install it into your phone for you and make sure it is all fully working. If you need any more information or want to see other deals or even just read up a bit more information it can all be found on their websites just search the names, or if you want more help and information upon arriving in Australia just visit a local store and someone will help and assist you.

## Chapter 7-Medicare and Health

So one of the most important things to look after while your travelling is going to be your health, a lot of people don't think about it as it doesn't really seem like an important thing but trust me, it is. You don't want to be getting ill before a big trip or come down with the flu before a Skydive and if you do, your going want to be able to go to a doctor, get your prescription and get it sorted as soon as possible so you can get back out into the sun and enjoying your travels, rather than being stuck inside tucked up in bed and feeling sorry for yourself. If you do get ill, it's different to being ill at home. It's inevitable your going to get ill at some point during your travels but there's a few things you can do to make better of the situation. Your most likely going to be sharing a room with people in a hostel, if you do get ill it can get very annoying especially with people turning the lights on and making noise when all you want to do is sleep, I know it doesn't sound very pleasant. So make sure you have loads of water, headphones or earplugs and something to cover your eyes like an eye mask, this will help you get some sleep and recover much more quickly. Also make sure you've got whatever you need from the doctors and it's probably best to just stick it out and stay in bed until your feeling better as you don't want to make it worse and ruin even more of your trip.

How to best avoid getting sick while travelling:

- Wash your hands, I know it sounds basic but you would be really surprised the people who forget to do this and its such an easy way to catch germs and get ill.
- Try and stay active, keep exercising, there are obviously a range of

benefits to regularly exercising, like it's going to build up your immune system and make you less susceptible to illnesses.

- One VERY important thing, that a lot of people don't seem to find important, but wearing sun cream. This is incredibly important in Australia especially up north as the UV levels are extremely high and skin cancer is a serious problem, so make sure you keep re applying sun cream, wear a hat and cover yourself up if you find the sun too much.
- Make sure you get your vaccinations before you leave, which I will speak more about later on in the book.
- Protect yourself from Mosquito bites. So use a mosquito net if your in the outback or camping. It's also a good idea to take mosquito repellent spray, good air conditioned rooms are great as mosquitoes are attracted to hot temperatures.
- Finally simple things that just help keep your immune system strong, make sure you get sleep even though your going to be busy partying and doing stuff in the day getting enough sleep is also important. Drink a lot of water and stay hydrated especially when in the sun it can be easy to forget.

Vaccinations:

You don't really need any immunisations if your going to Australia, you just need to make sure all your primary courses and boosters are up to date. Other vaccines you might also want to consider are Japanese Encephalitis and tetanus. Japanese Encephalitis is carried in mosquitoes and risk is higher for long stay travellers in rural areas and tetanus is found in spores in soil worldwide and gets into cuts, burns and other wounds. I would just recommend going into or phoning your GP and booking an appointment with the nurse, tell her/him your going to Australia for a gap year and wherever else you're planning on going and she will give you all the necessary Jabs and make sure your all up to date before leaving. I would also get a printed out/copy of your vaccinations to take with you just in case you need it.

Medicare:

The Australian Government has signed Reciprocal Health Care Agreements with the United Kingdom, the Republic of Ireland, New Zealand, Sweden, the Netherlands, Finland, Belgium, Norway, Slovenia, Malta and Italy. These agreements entitle you to some subsidised health services for essential medical treatment while visiting Australia which is great and basically means you get some health care for free.

If you are a resident of New Zealand, the United Kingdom, the Republic of Ireland, Sweden, Finland or Norway, you are covered for the length of your stay in Australia.

If you are a visitor from Belgium, the Netherlands or Slovenia, you need your European Health Insurance card to enrol in Medicare. You are eligible until the expiry date shown on the card, or for the length of your authorised stay in Australia, if that is an earlier date.

If you are visiting from Malta or Italy, and you are a resident and citizen of those countries, you'll be covered by Medicare for a period of six months from the date of your arrival in Australia.

How it works:

You can get medical treatment in private doctors' practices and community health centres. Doctors in these practices charge for their services in one of the following ways.

1. The doctor bills Medicare directly.

You'll be asked to show your reciprocal health care card and sign a completed Medicare bulk bill form after seeing the doctor but you won't need to pay. Please note not all doctors bulk bill.

2. The doctor gives you a bill.

Doctors who don't bulk bill will ask you to pay a fee at the time of consultation. You can either pay the full bill, or lodge the unpaid bill with Medicare and claim it back afterwards.

Also if you get treated in hospital you wont be charged for any treatment or accommodation you simply just show your passport or your Medicare card.

Medical services not covered by Medicare:

- Medicine not subsidised under the PBS.
- Treatment arranged before your visit to Australia.
- Accommodation and medical treatment in a private hospital.
- Accommodation and medical treatment as a private patient in a public hospital.
- Ambulance services.
- Dental examinations and treatment (except specified items introduced for allied health services as part of the Chronic Disease Management (CDM) program).
- Physiotherapy, occupational therapy, speech therapy, eye therapy, chiropractic services, podiatry or psychology (except specified items introduced for allied health services as part of the CDM program.
- Acupuncture (unless part of a doctor's consultation).
- Glasses and contact lenses.
- Hearing aids and other appliances.

- The cost of prostheses.
- Medical costs for which someone else is responsible (for example a compensation insurer, an employer, a government or government authority).
- Medical services which are not clinically necessary.
- Surgery solely for cosmetic reasons.
- Examinations for life insurance, superannuation or membership of a friendly society.
- Eye therapy.
- Home nursing.

## Chapter 8-Travel Insurance

Travel insurance is always a big question and I would always recommend getting some sort of cover, because if the worst is to happen, it's good to know your covered and it's there and it could end up saving you a lot money. Without travel insurance you could find yourself with a massive bill that you just can't afford to pay that's why it's a necessity. The main question is what type of travel insurance do you get for a gap year. Well to be honest there are thousands of different companies that offer travel insurance and thousands of different prices and types of cover, ranging from as little as £30 to as much as £800. The real question is which one should you get and how much should you spend on it, also what to look for when buying travel insurance. Make sure you get cover for as long as your going to be travelling for. I'd usually just get 12 months or a little longer than however longer your planning on staying just in case. You can pay for your travel Insurance in different ways which is also useful if your not sure how long you are going to be travelling for so you can just pay upfront for a whole year or you can pay monthly which might end up costing you more but it gives you the opportunity to stop paying if you decide to leave.

So the main things I would look for when buying travel insurance and what is a must would be:

- Medical and health cover for an injury or sudden illness.
- 24-hour emergency service and assistance.
- Personal liability cover in case you're sued for causing injury or damaging someone else's property.
- Cover for having your possessions lost or stolen for example baggage on planes etc.
- Cover for the cancellation of your trip or having to cut it short.
- Extra cover for activities that are commonly excluded from standard policies especially if your planning on doing them and are on a gap year like rafting, jet skiing, surfing etc.

So that's about it for travel insurance I'm not going to list all the different types and costs as there are thousands and they really easy to find and sort out. I would recommend paying around £100-£150 for travel insurance, just make sure all of the things mentioned above are included and any extra stuff that you think you might need. If you want to be extra careful you can pay a bit more but its entirely up to you and dependent on what your budget is. Just make sure you get some sort of cover before you leave the country and keep the email/conformation of your insurance, I would also read through the fine print before buying it as there may be some tricky little things in there so its always best to read through and make sure it is what it says. There are also a lot of comparison websites for travel insurance so you can refine what you are looking for and then compare them, this is what I would personally recommend, this saves you a lot of time and searching, then you can just pick which one suits you best.

## Chapter 9-Where to live?

So after sorting all of your necessities out and after spending your first week or so in a hostel, your going to want to find somewhere to live, maybe for a while or maybe just for the short term it entirely depends on your plans but there are lots of options.

Hostels:

So a hostel would probably be your first choice when arriving in a new country. They are great for meeting new people as everyone in them is in a similar situation to you, they are also great for partying, getting settled into a new place and getting a feel for the place. Hostels in Australia are pretty expensive and if your staying in them long term it would definitely be cheaper to get an apartment. Dorm rooms in Sydney range from around $20-$40 so your looking at around $175 for a week, you obviously get what you pay for. You may have to pay for Wifi which is another added extra cost. A Dorm room for those of you that don't know is a shared room where you share with other people, ranging from 4 people to 32 people the most common is 8 people dorms they can also be mixed or male and female. Obviously the more people the cheaper the room, but probably less sleep. Hostels have showers, kitchens, toilets, communal/chill out areas and are all in all a lot of fun. I absolutely loved living in hostels when travelling always meeting new people and always something to do and there's usually a party going on it really is great, but if your working then it can be difficult getting sleep and may not be the best choice but once again it is a lot of fun. A good website for booking hostels is www.hostelbookers.com you just enter the place you want to stay and an arrival date and it will give you a list of available hostels.

Apartments:

Your other choice is to get an apartment. Once again apartments range in prices and styles but you get a lot more flexibility and they are often a lot cheaper. It is entirely up to you what kind of apartment you get, you can get shared room apartments which is where you share a room with other people, this is what I ended up choosing. There are benefits and disadvantages to having a shared room apartment, one is that you are meeting new people again as you have them in your room. It's usually set out with 2 bunk beds in a room so four people and is a lot of fun, also giving you the chance to settle down if your staying somewhere for a while. It allows you to unpack all your stuff into cupboards, usually all bills are included, you get free unlimited Wifi and it's usually a lot cheaper, they range from $100 a week to about $170 obviously the more you pay the nicer its going to be and more room your going to have. With apartments you do have to pay a bond these can also range in price so make sure you have some money which you can use to put down the bond, you do get this when you leave the apartment if it has not been damaged. Bonds are often 2 weeks rent just to give you a rough idea. The other option for apartments is getting your own room this is obviously going to cost you more but gives you a lot more privacy, but then it doesn't have the same social aspect to it, so yeah it gives you that nice room to yourself which is nice but then your not with people and meeting as many new people and they are more expensive this is why by my choice I would go for a shared room. You can get your own room in an apartment with other people so it would be big house or apartment with say four private rooms which gives you your own privacy and the social aspect to a certain extent once again as you would be sharing a living room and kitchen but again these will cost more. Prices for your own room once again vary a lot depending on location and the room/ how big the apartment is. Again you get what you pay for but it can cost anywhere from $230-$500 per week obviously $500 a week being a very fancy room in a great location and would be a very nice place to live.

House:

The other option is getting a house with a group of people you have met or friends you may have gone travelling with. If there is a group of you all wanting to stay in the same city say 4-8 people you could rent a house and just divide the costs between you all. This can also be a lot of fun just a group of mates sharing a massive house. Once again prices range a lot but it's a good option if you want your own rooms and to share a kitchen and living area. Renting a house ranges on average from $500 to $2000 depending on location and number of bedrooms etc. Once again this may end up costing you a little more but you do get the privacy of your own room and a house to share with your friends.

How to find and Apartment?

There are quite a lot of options when it comes to finding an apartment and quite a few good places to look. If your staying in a hostel its always good to check the notice boards, they are often advertising for stuff like jobs, cars and apartments so have a look there and give them a call, you can even go and look in other hostels which your not staying in. There are other places to have a look online, www.gumtree.com.au is probably one of the main ones to find an apartment just search for say shared rooms in Sydney and then call the number and arrange and inspection. Another good website which I found is www.flatemates.com.au. This offers loads of different types of shared accommodation a lot of these are single rooms in a shared house but there are some that are very cheap and have good offers, for this website you do have to create an account, it's free though and then you just message them when you find a good room.

When you are looking for a room always go and inspect it first before you move in and check the terms make sure it includes all bills, Wifi, has washing facilities, oven, cupboard space, good shower etc. Then when you're happy with a place give them the bond and make sure you get a receipt and don't lose it so you know you can get your bond back when you leave and can prove it. Just a pre warning when in the cities be prepared to be a bit shocked at some of the shared rooms you will be viewing, there are some really nice ones and places that are good to live in, but there are some horrible ones like when I was looking in Sydney, I viewed a number of apartments where the sleeping areas were just a living room split up by curtains/sheets, they were crammed in and literally had no space, they were hard to even walk about in. But don't let that put you off as there are some really nice shared rooms that are good to live in. Also when staying in hostels ask around, ask people you meet if they know anyone or have got friends of people you can call this is always helpful and might help you find a nice place to stay.

## Chapter 10-Tax File Number (TFN)

When getting to Australia if you want to work you should apply for a tax file number. Everybody needs one to be able to work it's your personal reference number in the tax and super systems and is also an important part of your identity so you need to make sure that you keep it secure. When you get issued your TFN its yours for life, whether you change jobs, your name, or move overseas it always stays with you. You do not need a TFN to work in Australia but without it you will be taxed a lot more and wont be able to apply for any benefits, lodge your tax return online or apply for an Australian Business Number (ABN).

You can apply for a TFN online on the governments website www.ato.gov.au/Individuals/Tax-file-number and it's really easy to do. You can apply for a tax file number if you meet the their conditions, which are listed below:

- You are a foreign passport holder, permanent migrant or temporary visitor.

- You are already in Australia.
- Your visa is one of the following:
  - a permanent migrant visa.
  - a visa with work rights.
  - an overseas student visa.
  - a visa allowing you to stay in Australian indefinitely (including New Zealanders automatically granted a visa on arrival).

So if your going on a working holiday visa you can just apply when you get to Australia and then when you get a job give them your TFN. You will need to make sure you keep your TFN safe and write it down somewhere so that you always have it, write it in your notes as you will need it for every new job you get and when applying for tax back.

What if you can't find your TFN?

- Look on an income tax assessment or any other letter from the tax authorities.
- Look on your payment summary provided by your employer or your superannuation statement.
- Ask your Tax agent if you have one.
- Or call 13 28 61 between 8am to 6pm Monday to Friday.

## Chapter 11-Getting a Job

So when it comes to applying for a job in Australia everybody is going to have a different experience as there are thousands of different jobs available, some people find it easy getting a job others struggle, it entirely depends on what kind of job you're looking for and where you’re looking. When first applying for a Job in Australia you are going to have to get your work head on and get out of holiday mode for a bit as obviously the more work you put into finding a job the better chance you have of getting one a lot quicker. The minimum wage in Australia is $17.29 or $659.90 per 38 hour week, so there is the potential to save a lot of money if you wanted to, and also a good thing to remember is whatever you're taxed you get back at the end of the financial year which is the 30th of June or when you leave the country.

Firstly, you're going to have to right a resume/CV it's often called different things in different countries in Australia they call it a resume. When it comes to writing your CV, if you're planning on getting a job as soon as you get to Australia, get one written up before you leave it saves you doing it when you get there and gives you more time to relax and enjoy your holiday. It also means you can start applying for jobs right away. The simplest thing to do when writing your Australian Resume is just use the information from your normal CV. I would search on Google for 'Australian resume templates' have a look through to get a rough idea of what they look like and pick a template which you think looks best and the most professional, then copy it putting in all your own information. Things you should make sure to include in your Australian Resume is all your contact details so they can get in touch, your nationality, languages that you speak and which visa you are on plus when your visa expires.

When working in Australia on a working holiday visa you can only work for any one employer for up to six months so this might be something you would want to take into consideration. Employers will know this so there is no point in applying for Permanent positions when applying I would apply for temporary and casual work.

Types of Jobs:

There are loads of different types of jobs you can get, some more common than others and some that are much easier to get than others. For some of the Jobs you will have to get a certificate which anyone can get you just have to go and do a little bit of training, anybody can do it but I will talk about these a bit further on. The main types of jobs which most people get when on a working holiday visa are; Bar work, Construction, Call Centres and Cafés this is what you will hear most people doing as they all pay well and are reasonably easy to get and there are lots of opportunities readily available for these jobs. There are obviously other jobs that are a lot more specific but they may be a little harder to get but if you have a degree or some specific qualifications then by all means have a go applying for them and if you get them or don't get them nothing is lost.

When applying for jobs you will often attend an interview, they may call you first and have a chat with you, and then ask you to attend an interview, and will let you know about the job from there, very similar to most of your home countries, it does vary dependant on the type of job. There is also farm work but this you will only be doing if you want your second year visa to Australia, and is a little bit different, I will talk more about this in chapter 3. I myself worked in a call centre for charities I found it a lot of fun and it was a good way to meet a lot of people and save a lot of money. I did this in Sydney for about 5 months. When applying for jobs/going for interviews try not to get one that is commission only based as you may struggle to make a lot of money, there are a lot of these offered in the city to backpackers and they are often face to face sales jobs and in order to make any reasonable amount of money, you have to sell a lot of products and these jobs can be very hard. So try to get a job with an hourly rate of pay and if they have commission/bonuses on top then that's always a benefit.

Certificates needed for Specific Jobs:

RSA (Responsible Service of Alcohol):

You will need to get an RSA certificate if you are working anywhere that serves alcohol. It is mandatory for any alcohol serving staff. The course takes one day to complete and is fairly easy it just goes through the safety of alcohol and who to serve it too. There is no age restriction to apply to do the course but you cannot serve alcohol unless you are over the age of 18. RSA courses differ dependent on which state you are in. They usually cost about $60 unless you are in NSW so that's Sydney and its surrounding area in which case it is $130. If you complete the Course in NSW it is valid for all states apart from Queensland and Victoria where you would have to do a different course. If doing your RSA in NSW and Victoria you cannot do it online and it has to be done in the classroom it takes about 6 hours. For Queensland it can be done online but is valid in all other states but Victoria and NSW. You can also do a course which is valid for all states but it is obviously going to cost a lot more. I would just do the RSA for where you wanted to work in a bar and stay and look for bars in that area for a while. More information on each particular state can be found online with just a quick google search. There are loads of different companies offering the courses too, so have a look around for the best price.

The Course requires that students can demonstrate their ability to:

- Understand and comply with the legal responsibilities associated with the service of alcohol and Harm Minimisation in New South Wales.
- Define a standard drink and understand their strengths.
- Understand the effects of alcohol on the community and individuals.
- Recognise how much alcohol customers have consumed.
- Help prevent under-age drinking.
- Control and limit violent and unnecessary behaviour of intoxicated customers.

•Demonstrate an understanding of the methods employed in training to improve customer service.
•Improve internal communication skills to enhance control and monitoring for improved focus on customer's welfare.
•Improve communication with patrons in order to competently advise options available.

White Card (Green card):
This is a one day course and will enable you to work on a building site in NSW, as it is required that everyone holds a current Occupational Health & Safety Certificate or "Green Card", as it is known in the industry. You have to be the minimum age of 14 to be able to complete the course. A WorkCover NSW Statement of Training will be issued upon successful completion of the course, allowing you to work immediately in all states of Australia. Your White Card will be mailed directly to your nominated address by WorkCover. If your a bit confused as to why it's referred to as a green card and a white card, it's because it used to be green but it is now white so if anybody asks you for either you know what they mean. To obtain the card you will need to attend a one day occupational health and safety course (OH&S course) with an accredited trainer.

The course involves lectures on site safety, how to keep the work environment safe and what to do in case you have an accident. The morning is normally spent studying with talks from your lecturer followed by a short assessment. Provided you have understood what you have been taught you should be able to pass relatively easily, I did not do this myself but knew a lot of people that did complete this. The temporary certificate is issued at the end of the day and you receive the official plastic card in the post. Fees do vary but it usually costs around the $100 mark dependent on who you do it with. If you are planning on working in construction you will probably have to get steel toe cap boots too.

You can also do the training online if you want to, it usually takes around 4-5 hours and you can stop and start it when you like, once completed you will need to send the required paperwork in the post and then the card will be sent to you via post. Your white card is also valid in all states which is really helpful.

RCG (Responsibility Services of Gambling):
If you are going to be working in a place with gambling machines, you will need a Responsible Conduct of Gambling (RCG). RCG is a mandatory course for all gambling machines operating staff. You can get this certificate after attending a 1-day training course. No age restrictions apply to do this course but you need to be at least 18 to work in areas of gambling. Upon completing the course you will be issued with a NSW Office of Liquor Gaming & Racing Interim Certificate for Responsible Conduct of Gambling (RCG), allowing you to work immediately in NSW. To obtain the RCG photo card, you will have to apply at an Australia Post outlet for the card. In NSW and Victoria you will have to attend a class session while all the other states you will be able to complete the course online. Once again prices do vary dependent on where you are and which course you pick but it will be around $60.

Where to find a Job:

When you begin looking for a job in Australia there are lots of options and opportunities, if you are looking for bar work, cafés, coffee shops or alike then one of the best ways would be to print of a load of Resumes and go handing them out around the city. By doing this you are showing your face you may be able to talk to them a little bit and let them know what your personality is like and give a good impression. You also get to see the city and see the area which you are living. When looking for a job in Australia as a backpacker you cant be too fussy I know we would all like that perfect job but in reality it's not that possible, yeah you can find a nice job that you enjoy and pays well but don't expect it too be too glamorous, after all your just trying to save some more money for your travels.

When looking for jobs, look on hostel notice boards you will see loads of jobs advertised for backpackers like maybe just a few days work or some casual employment which is always useful if you want just a few days work. In your hostel they may also have someone that is there to help you find a job and help you out, this is not in every hostel but in some of the bigger ones, go and talk to them and see what they have to offer and whether there are any jobs. Another thing is just get chatting to people, when in hostels you would be surprised at the amount of people who know someone who is looking for someone to work and it's a really good way to get in contact with a possible employer.

The other way to apply for jobs is online and there are loads of options. It's really easy when applying for jobs you can often just create accounts and a profile, attach your Resume and then just apply for jobs in seconds. There are loads of websites you can use when applying for jobs and I have listed the best ones below:

- www.seek.com.au/jobs- This website offers loads of different jobs, you can refine what you are looking for and apply in seconds, this is the website I found my job in a call centre through.
- www.jobsearch.gov.au- Once again similar to seek I never used this site myself but again there are lots of job options on this website.
- www.gumtree.com.au- Another website which I'm sure a lot of you are familiar with is gumtree. There will be lots of jobs opportunities on this website allowing you to call or email the employer, do be careful though as there are some fakes, make sure you check when you get a reply to confirm it's a legitimate company/employer especially when its farm work. Just check to see if its got a website or a Facebook page, ask for an address and check it out. Just be aware.
- www.taw.com.au- Another good website that allows you to create a resume and an online account, this website does cost money though I think it's around $50 for a year. There are lots of job opportunities on it and you can guarantee they are all legitimate. This is very useful when searching for Farm Jobs, but I do not think you need it when applying for jobs in the cities as there are lots of other websites that are free and just as good.

Another option you could look for is working for accommodation, this is a great way to save money on rent while just working a few hours a day. This is literally where you work maybe 2-3 hours cleaning or tidying up or some sort of work in the hostel and your accommodation will be paid for in return. You often get free drinks and stuff at the bars too. Hostels also have people which take people out to the local clubs, so if you like partying all you have to do is round everyone up every night and take them out to the bars/clubs. Doing this you get your free accommodation, get loads of free drinks and it's a fantastic way to meet people and great for partying in general. Just go asking around the hostels, the best place to start is the hostel your staying at and see if they have any places, and you may as well leave them your resume while you're there. There is also farm work but I will talk about that in chapter 3.

## Chapter 12-Tax Back and Superannuation

So your planning on going to Australia and working at least for some period of your time. When working in Australia, you will obviously pay tax just the same as in any other country. When you are a backpacker in Australia you can claim your tax back which is fantastic, all that extra money. Now there are two times in a year you can do this, you can either do it at the end of the financial year, so that will be July the 1st of each year, or when you leave Australia, which is when I did mine as it's a nice little amount of money for you to return home with. How much tax you get back will be dependent on various factors:

- The length of time you have been in the country.
- The amount of tax you have been paying.
- Your gross earnings.

There are various ways in which you can claim your tax back. Firstly you can do it by yourself this is quite a lengthy process and you could mess it up, but it could end up saving you $100-$200, it's entirely up to yourself if you want to try and claim it back on your own, but make sure you don't make any mistakes as it could end up costing you even more money, all the information about getting your tax back by yourself can be found on the governments website. There are also various companies that will claim your tax back for you, this is what I decided to do. There are hundreds of companies that specialise in claiming your tax back for you. I chose to use www.taxback.com they were incredibly helpful, all you have to do is fill in a simple form and send in copies of your payslips, which will show how much tax you have paid, they will also need a photocopy of your passport, but you can do all that in one of there offices which are located in most cities and even towns, after that it's done you just wait a few weeks and the money will be in your account. You can even do it all and apply online, without going into an office which is perfect if your on the move. They do take a fee for sorting and getting your tax back for you, it depends on how much money you are due, I was due about $5000 in tax back, and they charged me around $300.

So when you are in Australia make sure you keep all your payslips, some for example on farms you may get in paper form make sure you keep these so you can claim this tax back, others for jobs say in cities will be online just save them to a folder in your emails. For each employer you will only need the most recent one which shows the total tax you paid, but it's best to keep them all just in case. You can get your tax refund paid into any back account either into your Australian account or into an overseas account so it's there for when you arrive home. When applying for your tax refund you will also need your TFN, so make sure you have this to hand.

Superannuation is a little bit different, this is basically a percentage (9%) of your earnings set aside for when you retire, and if you are not a permanent resident in the country, you can claim it back when you leave. Again this can be done by yourself, but it's a lengthy processes which you probably wont want to be doing when your travelling, or you can use one of the many companies that can arrange and do it all for you. Again I used www.taxback.com to get my super back the same as I used for my tax return. With your superannuation, you can get it all applied for and set up before you leave Australia after you have finished working, you can even apply for it online the same as with your tax back, but you have to wait until you have been out of Australia for 6 months until you can receive it, which is quite a long time but they need to make sure you are not returning. You will also need various other documents when you claim your superannuation, such as signed copies of your passport by specific people in both Australia and your home country, as well as payslips and any other information they ask for. Again you can get this sent into your home bank account so make sure they have your bank account details which they probably will have from doing your tax return. Getting your superannuation back is a much more lengthy process than getting your tax so be prepared to wait.

I would recommend before you leave going into a tax back office and asking them about it, they will give you all the forms required and documents that you need to sign to get it sorted before you leave Australia. Then it's done and you don't have to worry about it, you will also know you have a nice little amount of money coming in six months after being home from Australia. You can still return to Australia on another visa if you claim your superannuation also.

# Visas and Farm Work

## Chapter 13-Getting a Visa

So when planning your trip to Australia one of the first things you are going to need to think about before you even think about anything else is getting a visa, because without this your not even going to be able to step foot in the country. There are a range of places you can buy your visas from and a range of different companies but I would just get it from the official government website to be sure and safe. You just set up an account with them and then apply and pay for your visa. They are usually pretty quick with getting back to you I got offered my working holiday visa in under 24 hours after applying. When your visa gets accepted before you leave I would print a copy of all the documents from your visa to take with you in your hand luggage so if they ask you for them, you have them to hand. Sometimes they may ask you about funds and how you plan on funding yourself but just give them honest answers and they will have no reason not to let you into the country. I had no problems at all when going through customs it literally took 10 minutes. Also when applying for your visa make sure you have at least 6 months left on your passport from when you plan on leaving the country as they may not let you enter if you don't. When I applied I did not realise but I got my visa accepted and then noticed I didn't have 6 months from when I would be leaving the country, this was no problem at all though as they just asked for my new passport number and contacted me when it was all changed and sorted. Visas for Australia are also electronic so you don't get sent a sticker or have to send your passport off it's all done by microchips you will just get stamp when you go through customs when you arrive. There a couple types of visa that I will mention and talk about that you may want to get when visiting Australia. The first is a tourist visa: You can get a tourist visa if you don't plan on working while you are in Australia. Which for many of you going on a gap year you wont want, but I'll mention it anyway.

There are two types of tourist visa.

1.)Visitor visa (subclass 651) which is valid for 3 month entries over a period of 12 months. It is free and you can apply online you can find more more information and apply on the government website
www.immi.gov.au/visitors/tourist/evisitor
Or

2.) Tourist visa (subclass 676), which allows you to stay for up to 12 months. You have to pay for this visa once again you can apply and find more information here on the governments website
www.immi.gov.au/visitors/tourist/676/

The other type of visa which a lot of people going on a gap year will get is a working holiday visa (subclass 417), this allows you to work in Australia for any employer for up to 6 months you can work for 12 months but it would have to be with two separate employers. You are also not allowed to study for a period of 4 months or more. The visa can take up to 8 weeks to process but it shouldn't take that long, it depends on your situation. You can apply for this visa online it takes about 30 minutes. You can apply online and find more information here at this link https://www.border.gov.au/Trav/Visa-1/417-. All you have to do is set up an Immi account fill in all your details and give them the information they need. Then pay for your visa and they will get back to you once it has been accepted and give you a visa reference number by email. When you have this visa you can leave and go to Australia as many times as you like within the 12 months, and the visa starts from the date/time when you first enter Australia and lasts for 12 months then on. The working holiday visa to Australia costs $420 dollars approximately £250. When applying for a working holiday visa there are certain requirements which you have to meet to be able to apply:

- Must be between the age of 18-30.
- Must have a valid passport with at least 6 months until renewal.
- You must have sufficient funds to be able to support yourself when in Australia.
- You must not have any substantial criminal convictions.
- You must not have any substantial medical issues.
- Will not be accompanied by a dependent child at any point during your stay.

You can only apply for a working holiday visa if you are from one of the countries stated below, you can also get a working holiday visa if you are from the United States, it is very similar but differs slightly with some of its conditions.

Eligible Passport Holders

- Australia currently has reciprocal working holiday arrangements with:

| | | |
|---|---|---|
| Belgium | Canada | Denmark |
| Estonia | Finland | France |
| Germany | Hong Kong* | Italy |
| Japan | Malta | Norway |
| Republic of Cyprus** | Republic of Ireland | Republic of Korea |
| Sweden | Taiwan | The Netherlands |
| United Kingdom | | |

*Hong Kong Special Administrative Region of the People's Republic of China

**Holders of passports from The Republic of Cyprus are not eligible to apply for an electronic working holiday visa, and must lodge their application with their resident Australian Government office.

There are a lot of other visas on offer for specific jobs, students etc. But these are the main two that you might want to use if you are going on a gap year to Australia. The others are often specific to professional careers if you do want any more information on visas or immigration just visit the government website www.border.gov.au/.

## Chapter 14-Getting a Second Year Visa

So once your in Australia if you choose to use a working holiday visa you can apply for second year working holiday visa which entitles you to another whole year in Australia. There are certain requirements and things which you have to do to be able to obtain this visa, such as your regional farm work, but I will talk about farm work and where to get it in the next section this is just specifically about the second year visa itself. The second year visa is basically exactly the same as the first working holiday visa in regards to working and studying etc.

The requirements are also exactly the same as the first working holiday visa apart from you would have had to undertake 3 months or 88 days of specified regional farm work. You can apply for a second year visa when your in or out of Australia but if your out of Australia when applying then when the visa is granted you must be out of Australia and the same if you are in Australia. The average processing time for the second year visa is from 2-6 weeks so when you apply if you are in Australia you should make sure you have at least 28 days left on your first visa when you apply for your second year. If you are out of the country it doesn't matter too much. Once your application has been granted, you will have one year to activate the visa; you can do this by simply entering Australia. Alternatively, if you are in Australia when you lodge your application and do not leave, your second year visa will automatically come into effect when your first year application expires. The second year visa costs £295 so is quite expensive but it does allow you to stay in Australia for another year. When your second year visa has been granted you will receive an email confirming this and confirming that everything has been approved and your second year visa application successful. When you do your farm work for your second year visa, if you complete your farm work after the 31st of August 2015 you will need to provide payslip evidence as proof that you have worked on a farm. If you completed your farm work before this date or were mid way through it on this date you do not need payslip evidence. When submitting for your visa other evidence to include to prove you completed your farm work would be things like bus tickets, accommodation slips, group certificates and tax returns these are just some examples that may help speed up your application.

## Chapter 15-Farm/Regional Work

So as you now know, if you complete your 3 months regional farm work, you can get a second year visa to Australia. There are loads of different types of jobs available depending on what kind of work your looking for the pay, accommodation, work hours it all varies. Some are family run farms where it will just be you helping out a family, others are there may be 20 other backpackers and you will all be working together. Farm work is hard and it can be very physical, again it depends on specifically what type of farm job you get. I myself had 2 farm jobs so split up my 88 days, I did half on a farm in Queensland picking Zucchinis, there were about 20 other people all doing this, it was very hard work in the sun just walking down a field picking vegetables. And the other farm was a family run horse farm this was a bit more fun and a better experience as I would do a range of things, such as look after horses, fencing, ride quad bikes, put out hay, general maintenance work etc. Both were completely different experiences and both taught me a great deal. I would definitely recommenced splitting it up though and doing half on one farm and half on another as this gives you the chance to get two different experiences, and then you wont get as bored as get the two opportunities, but then again if you are enjoying your first farm so much then stay for sure.

Types of Farm Jobs/Specified Work:

So there are lots of different types of farm jobs that count as specified work and it can be done in a range of areas.

Plant and Animal Cultivation:

- Cultivating or propagating plants, fungi or their products or parts.
- General maintenance crop work.
- Harvesting and/or packing fruit and vegetable crops.
- Immediate processing of animal products including shearing, butchery in an abattoir, packing and tanning.
- Immediate processing of plant products.
- Maintaining animals for the purpose of selling them or their bodily produce, including natural increase.

- Manufacturing dairy produce from raw material.
- Pruning and trimming vines and trees.

Fishing and Pearling:

- Conducting operations relating directly to taking or catching fish and other aquatic species.
- Conducting operations relating directly to taking or culturing pearls or pearl shell.

Tree Farming and Felling:

- Felling trees in a plantation or forest.
- Planting or tending trees in a plantation or forest that are intended to be felled.
- Transporting trees or parts of trees that were felled in a plantation or forest to the place where they are first to be milled or processed or from which they are to be transported to the place where they are to be milled or processed.

Mining:

- Coal mining.
- Oil and gas extraction.
- Metal ore mining.
- Non-metallic mineral mining and quarrying.
- Exploration and other mining support services.

- Construction:
- Building construction.
- Heavy and civil engineering construction.

- Construction services.

When completing your farm work it has to be done in a regional area, regional Australia is any area outside of Sydney, Newcastle, Wollongong, the NSW Central Coast, Brisbane, the Gold Coast, Perth, Melbourne or the ACT. Regional Australia is defined by specific postcodes. some states such as South Australia and Tasmania count as regional Australia in their entirety, while others such as Western Australia simply require you to avoid the more populated areas like Perth.

*(Farm Work in Ayr, Queensland. Zucchini Picking)*

Where to Find Farm Jobs?

So when looking for a farm job there are lots of places to look and ways of finding legitimate farm work so you can get your second year visa. Similar to looking for a normal job you can go and have a look around hostels and on notice boards. There are often advertisements for farm work on the jobs boards in hostels so it is worth going and having a look. Once again asking around is always a good idea, people may have been on good farms and maybe able to give you a contact number for you to call and get more information etc. There are also a few websites which you can use to find farm work:

- http://www.taw.com.au/ - This is a good website everything on here is legitimate so you don't have to worry about getting a dodgy farm that wont be able to sign you off, as it's all run through the website. There is a sign up fee as mentioned previously it's about $50 for the whole year. This is where I found my job for zucchini picking, its a good website you can just attach your CV, and then apply for jobs with the click of a button.
- http://www.gumtree.com.au/ - Gumtree in my opinion is a fantastic website if your looking farm work, there are thousands of listings all with different types of farm work, from cattle farms, dairy farms, fruit picking, mining, oysters and so many more so you can refine your search. It's really easy to apply again you just attach your CV and leave a bit of a covering note telling them how many days you have left to complete of your farm work and why you want the job. Gumtree is where I found the horse farm which I worked on. With Gumtree though make sure you check up on the farms like there address, see if they have facebook pictures any reviews etc. Personally I would do this with any website, just to confirm its legitimacy and it enables you to gain an idea of what it's like.
- http://jobsearch.gov.au/harvesttrail/towncroplist.aspx – This is the governments website for harvest work. You can either search by month or by state. It gives you lists of all of the different types of vegetables and fruits that you can pick the months they are in season and places work is available. It then gives you information about the places and jobs, and you can call or email them with the details provided. I never used this

website personally, but it's great for information on when harvesting and picking work is available. This website is just picking though there is no horse or cattle farms if you are looking for something like that.

There are also a few other websites out there that you can use but these are the main three I would stick to. You can find it in other places, just have a browse online and see what you can find until you find one you like or a good website. I would definitely recommend Gumtree though as there is so much variety and choice and it gives you a chance to get a look at all the different types of farms and opportunities on offer.

Precautions to take when looking for farm work:
When you are planning on completing your farm work and applying for jobs you are going to want to take some precautions. I wouldn't worry about taking these precautions when applying for jobs just apply for all of the ones that suit your interests and you think that you would like. When you start to get responses from the farms and start deciding which ones you want to go to that is when you need to take precaution to find out if it is everything it says it is and is legitimate.
Precautions to take and things to find out before you leave for a farm:

- The address and name of the farm, get an address and find out where it is, search it up on Google maps, see if it looks all legitimate search the name of the farm on Google to see if they have a website or a Facebook page. Some may not but it's good to check up and have a look at pictures of the farm and reviews. And have a look at the local area see what it's like for shops etc.
- What do they pay, you need to make sure you know what your getting paid, is it per hour, for the week, or per the bucket.
- Accommodation so where you will be staying, is it going to be a shared room or your own room is there cooking equipment or is your food

provided which it often is if your working on a family run farm. Laundry facilities and will there be Wifi, but bare in mind that very often on the farms they are in the middle of nowhere and may not have Wifi or even signal at all so let your family and friends know where you are going and for how long you plan on being there.

- Transport, you need to know how you will get there, so how long it will take and whether you have to get a bus or train etc.
- Also find out how long a typical day of work is and the hours you are going to be expected to work.
- It also very important to find out how long the work is going to last for so are you planning on staying there the full three months or half say 40 days you need to let them know before you go on the farm and that this is okay with them.
- Another thing which isn't necessary but may be nice to have and know is find out if there are any other people on the farm, where they are from. And ask for some pictures, it's always nice to have some pictures of the farm you are going to be staying on before you go so you can see what it looks like and where you will be staying.

Types of Accommodation:

Accommodation options vary massively when doing your farm work. What is very popular is something called a working hostel which is just like a backpacker hostel. These hostels have connections with a range of local farmers, and then the hostels will find work for you through these farms. They often provide transport too. This is a much more social kind of farm work, I did not do it myself but I know a lot of people that did that really enjoyed it, it is a lot more physical the work as you will be doing work like picking fruit and vegetables. You pay for the accommodation but then you also get paid for the work you do. With this is may take longer than expected though as there is not always work available on specific days. Other types of accommodation vary again it depends on the type farm work. It may be independently run like a family farm you may have your own room and share a house with a couple other workers. Or it may just be you living in the farm owners house in the spare room, so with the family, it's best to have a look and see what is offered with particular jobs.

*(Farm Work in Margaret River, Western Australia. Horse Farm)*

What you get when you finish?

When you finish you will get a print out of the second year working visa holiday form 1263, when you get this you need to make sure it is all fully filled out with the farms contact details such as address and telephone number and the employers ABN number which is the number you have if you own your own business in Australia, and obviously their signature. Also make sure that they put the amount of days you worked and then the rest of the information you fill in yourself. Here is a link to what the form looks like when you get it.
https://www.border.gov.au/Forms/Documents/1263.pdf

## Chapter 16-Living Permanently in Australia

After spending a year in Australia and maybe even starting your second year, you may have fallen in love with the country like I did and decide that you want to live there permanently. There a few ways in which you can live there after you complete your second working holiday visa but it can be complicated and is not an easy thing to do. I have never done this myself so I am not talking from experience here. I am talking from what people I know have said to me from their experiences and from research online. Here are the few ways in which you can stay in Australia for the long term:

- Skilled Independent Visa (sub Class 175)- This is the quickest way to become a permanent resident in Australia. As it will allow you to become a permanent resident as soon as it is issued, but it's more complicated than that and to acquire this you will have to have a certain skill set. Designed for skilled migrants who have expertise in industries that are in a shortage in Australia. The process is very complex and takes a long time up to 12 months and you will be required to have your skills assessed by an independent body. In order to qualify you must be skilled, and have extensive experience in an industry in demand as per the skills shortage list, be under 45 and score at least 120 points on the general points test. If English is not your first language then you will also have to pass the IELTS test to show you have competent level of English. There are many benefits to this visa such as you attain permanent residency immediately and can also migrate with your partner and any children you may have.

- Employer Sponsored- A very popular visa with backpackers and an easier way to remain long term in Australia is to be sponsored by an employer.

You must work in a certain skilled occupation in Australia and the employer must be willing to sponsor you. Your employer will then nominate you to a position and provide evidence of your relevant skills and reasons as to why you are most suitable to the position. Other requirements are that you will need to attain a certain set wage for the occupation and meet health and English language standards. If you are planning on being sponsored it is best to get looking as soon as possible say when you start your second year visa as this gives you a better chance of finding sponsorship and saves you being let down and not being able to find a sponsor. The company will often sponsor you for a certain period and you should apply and get a 457 skilled Visa which allows you to stay in the country for up to 4 years, the process is different for each applicant depending on what you're being sponsored for. After your four years on the 457 visa you can apply for another four years but you should consider applying for the Permanent resident visa.

- Set up a Business- Another way is you can set up your own business, this may allow you to stay in Australia. Australia is keen to attract overseas money and also skilled businesses and Business people. It is a two stage process where you will be permitted a set amount of time to build the business as a temporary resident. If after this time, normally 4 years, you are generating enough revenue or employing Australians or both you may well then be granted permanent residency. Again if you conduct your business in a regional area you may be considered more favourably. This is quite a complicated process on getting this visa and there are varying sub-classes.

- Get Married- If you have ended up meeting the love of your life while in Australia or on your working holiday visa then you may be able to apply for a spouse visa. You must be in an ongoing relationship with a permanent resident or Australian citizen to be considered. If you are in a genuine relationship and have been for a minimum of 12 months then this is probably one of the easier options and will mean that you will be granted temporary residency for 2 years. After 2 years if you can show you are still together then you will more than likely be granted permanent residency.

If you are planning on living in Australia permanently after doing a working holiday and find you fall in love with the place, then do some research way before your visa runs out, plan how you are going to be able to stay in the country and what options you have this will save you a lot of stress and allow you to be prepared and have an idea of what you need to do to be able to live there and save you disappointment. There are some other options if you wish to stay in Australia for longer than your 2 year working holiday visa allows you, like getting a student visa and all this information is available on the government website, http://www.border.gov.au/.

One last piece of advice, make sure you do not overstay your visa time. As immigration will eventually catch up with you and you will end up being deported and will receive a ban to the country for a few years. This may also affect any other future visa applications to Australia and any other countries, and you may as well say goodbye to your dream of living in Australia.

## Hostels and Introduction Packages

### Chapter 17-Hostel Life

So what's hostel life all about? I did speak a little bit about hostels in the where to live chapter saying how much they cost and what you should expect from them, but this will go into a little more detail. When travelling you will probably spend most of your time in hostels as they are the cheapest places to stay short term in consideration to hotels and motels. They are often just as cheap as camp sites too. They also offer a fantastic social aspect and are brilliant for meeting new people as long as you put yourself forward and are not too shy. Staying in hostels gives you this opportunity to be able to talk to new people from all different nationalities and backgrounds, and gives you the chance to learn about different events and travel opportunities that otherwise you may not have found out about.

If this is your first time travelling or the first time that you are planning on staying in a hostel then be prepared, it's totally different to staying in a hotel. You will get used to it after a week maybe quicker such as getting used to sleeping with other people in the room, and maybe not getting much sleep for the first week until you get used to the noise, as hostels can be noisy places with music pumping until 11-12pm, and drunk people entering the room at all hours in the morning. People snoring is also horrific, luckily I didn't encounter this very often but if you get a heavy snorer in the room it can be very annoying and hard to get sleep. Another thing to mention as it may be a shock to you when first staying in hostels is yes sex in dorms does happen, regularly, yep the whole bed squeaking, moans and awkward hellos in the morning is all a part of hostel life most people that have stayed in hostels a while know it happens and yes it's another thing you'll have to get used to.

Eating in hostels is great, it's a good way to socialise and meet new people when you are in the kitchen. Kitchens in hostels range in sizes I've had them where they have been incredibly small with just a couple hobs between 40 people and huge kitchens where there's always space, just make sure you wash and clean the stuff you have used when you've done for others. Also when in hostels when buying your food, you are going to want somewhere to keep it all, they do have fridges in hostels but you need to put your food in a bag, a lot of people buy big cool bags and put all there food in them, I just used the carrier bags from the supermarket and label them with your name, room number and the date you are leaving. If you don't when the cleaners clean the fridges they will chuck out your food, which lets face it none of us want. Another thing to mention for when planning to cook, around 5-7pm the kitchens will be very busy with everybody all wanting to eat there dinner, so if you don't want to wait for a stove probably just go a bit later or earlier to cook then you won't be waiting around for somewhere to cook, hopefully.

Something we all hate to mention as backpackers is the thought of bed bugs. I never encountered bed bugs in a hostel during my travels and this was through Asia as well maybe I just got lucky or maybe there just some hyped up fear. But yes occasionally you do get bed bugs in hostel beds, I wouldn’t worry about it though or let it put you off staying in hostels it rarely happens and if you do get them, just mention it to a member of staff, you’ll probably get a refund and they’ll move you beds.

Then there’s other things like Wifi, often in smaller hostels the Wifi is free surprisingly it's usually the cheaper hostels that include free Wifi, and sometimes even free computers for you to use. Though some hostels may charge you say for every 20 minutes of internet time you use. You can also often print stuff off at hostels they will obviously charge you for this, but it will be no more than 50c for a sheet, which is useful to know if you need to print out flight information or copies of visas etc. Hostels also have places where you can do you laundry, once again this is going to be at an extra charge and how you do it varies from hostel to hostel sometimes they have a big room with washing machines in where you go and do it yourself and then hang it up to dry or put it in a dryer. Other hostels you just put it all in a bag with your name and room number on it and give it to the reception and they will, wash and dry it for you and give it back to you the next day. It usually costs around $5 to wash and dry all your clothes, and sometimes it is done on weight so will cost you so much per KG.

That's about it from hostels other than that, enjoy it and get involved with what everybody else is doing at nights, introduce yourself. In many hostels in the evenings pretty much every night, they have people that work at the hostels getting everyone up and partying, and they play drinking games like beer pong, flip cup and loads of others, although they are two of the favourites. So go and get involved, make the most of it and chat to people, and you'll end up having a great time. Just a pre warning, some of the more commercial hostels, usually the ones with their own bars don't allow you to bring alcohol in and if they catch you with any they will take it off you, you will have to buy it from the bar, I usually found this a lot less fun as there was less of a social aspect from the hostel, the better hostels in my opinion were the smaller ones, as they let you bring in your own alcohol and everybody knows each other it's more of a family like hostel, so if I were you I would definitely not book into one of the big hostels and book into a smaller one as there a lot more fun and sociable.

## Chapter 18-Meeting New People

Now if you've been travelling before then this won't really affect you as you will know what it's like and how easy and fun it is to meet new people when travelling. But if your a first time traveller and haven't stayed in hostels before then the prospect of going on your own can be a bit daunting, even if your going with a friend, you don't just want it to be you two the whole trip do you? Of course your going to want to get chatting to new people, that's all in the experience of travelling. Now a lot of you may think it's not that important the meeting of new people, but from my experience it's often not only the places you visit but the people you visit them with, this can make a huge difference to the experience of the trip and make it so much more fun and a much greater memory. Often the places that stand out most in my memories are the places I went with the best people. The obvious best way to meet new people when travelling is to just talk to people and get chatting about where your from, where your going, how long you've been travelling etc. But here's a few more ways if you're a bit worried about it and way of getting to know people and get a group of people to hang out with while travelling:

1. Carry a pack of cards- Now this may sound like a really simple thing but if you see a couple of people drinking in your hostel or even just sat around at night not drinking, even though highly unlikely in a hostel. You can just ask if they want to play cards, or know any good drinking games, the majority of people know some card games and it always makes drinking more fun. This is a great way to get to know people, you can introduce yourself, learn card games from each others countries, and before you know it everyone's having a good time and it's like you've been friends for ages. This is great for anywhere from hostels, to bars even on trains when you've got a long journey and everyone's bored as hell.
2. Ask people questions- people in your hostels, in your room, at the a the bar, ask them things such as where is good to visit around here, what are some good places to see or what are you guys doing tomorrow. Have a chat about their recommendations, and what their plans are while they're staying in the same place as you, then maybe you can do them together and you will already have a friend for the next day to do something with and maybe make future plans with.
3. Go on a tour- If you really are nervous or worried about the whole thing, go on a tour. There will be loads of people to talk to and the tour will usually get people talking anyway, it's a great way to meet new people and you'll have a lot of fun doing them as well.
4. Be flexible with your plans- Everybody will usually have a schedule or at least a rough idea of where they want to go on their travels, and the places they want to see, but you need to be able to be flexible and it can lead to an even better trip than expected. So many times when I was travelling I would have plans and then meet a few people and they would

have different plans, so I would join them and do what they were doing and it turned out to be incredible, some of the best parts of my travels happened by doing this, and it's a great way to meet new people and make the most of your trip. So do stuff that you didn't originally plan to do, it's where the greatest stories come from.

That is just a couple of ideas to help you meet new people if you are worried, but honestly there is no need to worry at all, there are going to be thousands of other people in exactly the same situation as you, all doing the same thing and looking to meet new people, honestly it's easy and you'll rarely not have someone to do stuff with, as long you be open minded and have a willingness to talk to people and be friendly you'll be fine. I remember meeting people in Australia and then randomly bumping into them again in Thailand, or I met someone in Thailand and then randomly bumped into them again in a small town in Vietnam, it really is crazy. Also when you do meet people and spend some time travelling with them even just for a day, get there contact details, Facebook is great for this and if you ever see that they are in the same place as you, you can always hit them up and plan to meet again.

## Chapter 19-Security/Travel Safety

When travelling your security and safety is obviously going to be extremely important. I think it's mainly about being in the wrong place at the wrong time, and it's the same with everywhere you go, as I'm sure even in your home town, you get your good places and your bad places. Not only that but when travelling you often carry as little as possible, as this is going to make your life easier. Which means everything you have in your rucksack is essential so it's really important you look after your things and try your best not to lose things, some stuff we could cope with losing like a pair of socks or a t-shirt but others such as a passport, mobile phone or wallet would affect your travel experience. Here's a few tips on how to make your trip less stressful and make sure everything's is backed up and secure:

- Double Check- Make sure you double check when you leave somewhere, this may be a bus, a hostel or even a café you sat in just very briefly. I don't mean go rummaging through your whole backpack counting your pants, but make sure you have the essentials, Passport, Phone, Wallet, Laptop and any bus/plane/train tickets you might need. And at least if you double check where you were sitting you will be able to see that you haven't left anything.
- Keep your source of money in different places- This means not leaving all of your bank cards or cash in your wallet as then if you lose your wallet, you're screwed. But leave them in different places so in your folder in your rucksack, your wallet, a sock etc. So then if you do lose one it's not the end of the world. Also when travelling I would keep some spare money in your rucksack just in case say $100 dollars, as you never know when you might need cash, and if you do use it, don't forget to replace it.
- Scan all your major documents- This means scan your passport mainly as if you lose your passport, then it can be a huge hassle and have major implications on the rest of your trip. At least if you have a photocopy you can take it to the UK embassy and get it sorted out and a temporary passport much quicker. But you may also want to scan other documents like, driving license, visas, travel insurance. You may be thinking why do I need all these paper copies it's all on my computer or phone, but what if you lose these and can't get to a computer, so it's best to have them digitally saved and paper based. You will most probably never need them, but better safe than sorry right.

- Don't leave items unattended- Now this may seem obvious, and it's not something you have to worry about greatly especially in Australia, I used to leave my bag on the beach and go surfing and come back and never had any problems, but just use precaution, make sure you leave it in sight so you can see it, at the end of the day it's your own risk.
- When I was travelling and staying in hostels I always used to put the most important things in my pillow case, so say my passport, phone, wallet etc. If you get into a habit of doing this it can save a lot of stress as then you will always know where it is, or use safety deposit boxes if they have them. But for example after night out when you get in put everything back in your pillow case and then when you wake up you will just be in a habit of knowing it's there and won't be stressing out looking for your passport checking every pocket of your clothing in the morning.
- Put it Away- Now this may also seem obvious but don't leave expensive things lying around on your bed, like laptops, phones or tablets. Yes if you do 90% of the time it is going to be fine as generally travellers don't steal of each other and show respect, but you always get the few that don't, so don't get caught out and just put it back in your bag or rucksack when you've finished using it.
- Washing- Now this may sound like a strange one and no I don't mean as in washing yourself. As in washing your clothes. I unfortunately did have a bad experience with this, it wasn't the end of the world as was only clothes but still an unnecessary cost, and left me short for a few days. When in warmer places you will wash your clothes and often hang them out to dry on communal washing lines to save you the cost of drying them in the machine. It's up to you, you don't hear of people having clothes stolen of washing lines often but it does happen, as it did to me, leaving me with nothing but my underwear and the clothes I was wearing. You could just use a dryer and not leave the possibility but just

so you know it happens, and take precaution.

That's about it for security and keeping safe when your backpacking, it's mainly just using your common sense as you would when you go anywhere even in your home town. But it's obviously a bit more important when travelling as that's all you have with you and everything you own is important. You can buy stuff such as padlocks to lock up your backpack when you go out, but I wouldn't worry about it too much I used one for the first 2 weeks and then you tend to stop as realize hostels are generally a safe place to leave your stuff. Most hostel rooms will have a security deposit box in anyway which you can lock shut with your own padlock, so if they have them just put all your valuables inside, and don't forget to bring a padlock for the security deposit boxes. I would also recommend getting one with a code, not a key, as if you lose the key it can be very annoying, this happened to my friend in Bali, which means having someone to come and open the locker with bolt cutters, and losing a little key is easily done and it's something else to worry about losing.

## Chapter 20-Intro Packages Advantages and Disadvantages

If your planning a working holiday visa to Australia and you've already done a little bit of research then you've probably heard of these intro packages that are available. There are a lot of companies out there that have them and they range in prices and what they offer you. First time travellers often decide to book a package as they sort everything out for you such as your TFN, bank account, sim card, they also set you up with your first weeks worth of activities seeing the place you decide to start. There are also a lot of other people doing these intro packages and if you are on your own then it's a great way to meet new people when first arriving in Australia, these do come at a price though and can cost quite a lot of money. When I first arrived in Australia I did an intro package with

Ultimate Oz, and I had a lot of fun, but I didn't really feel it was worth what I paid for it and that I could have done a lot of it myself very easily which I did end up doing. I will go through a couple of Intro packages explaining what they offer and there costs, and then list in my opinion the advantages and disadvantages of these intro packages and what I would recommend.

*(Ultimate Oz Group, Sydney)*

There are two popular intro packages for Australia which you may have come across, Oz Intro and Ultimate Oz, what they offer is below:

Ultimate Oz:

- They offer you pre departure support which I thought was useful, if I needed any help before I left instead of trawling the web, I would often just email these guys.

- They offer you easy arrival, so someone waiting for you and they will drop you off at your hostel when you land, and your hostel is booked for you. In my opinion it's actually easier to do this yourself and will be quicker, like getting a train to the city is cheap and fast, a lot of hostels offer free shuttles anyway. I was waiting like 40 minutes for my shuttle to leave as there were not enough people.
- They sort you out with an Australian Bank account which is good as they open it for you before and you can just transfer money before you leave. But you can do this online by yourself it literally takes five minutes and then you just go into a bank in Australia with your passport and confirm it, and you can still transfer money this way.
- Sim card they sort out for you, once again super easy to do by yourself just go into any phone store ask what deals they have and then they will give you one. The original Sim card that was offered to me, I didn't even us and ended up getting a completely different one, as found a cheaper better alternative.
- They will also sort you out with a TFN for when you arrive but again, you can apply for one of these yourself in about five minutes.
- Mail Service, this I did find very useful, if you receive any mail while you are in Australia you can get it sent here. They will then scan it in if it's a letter and you can log into your online mail account and read it which is great if you are travelling. They also hold your actual mail so if you get a parcel, then you can go and collect it whenever is convenient.
- They will also help you sort out your Tax refund for when you leave Australia which is basically when you work you get taxed and they will help you claim this back when you leave Australia, at a cost of course. I just did this through a company called Taxback.com.au and it was extremely easy to do they just charge you a small fee and it's done.

- They also give you a 12 month subscription to Travellers at work. This is a job website that allows you to apply for jobs in cities such as call centres and bars and also farm jobs. I used this quite a lot and found it very useful, but it is not a necessity really, you can find jobs easily enough on loads of other websites and if you really want you can sign yourself up for like $40.
- They also include in your package an RSA course which you may be thinking that's great that will be really useful if looking for bar work, but what I didn't realize until I arrived was that this is not valid for NSW which is Sydney, and this was where I wanted to live and work, so that was completely useless to me.

These are the main things that they offer and what I think to them and whether they are worth it or not, this is just my personal opinion, and this is just what one specific company offers, as said before there are a few companies out there that do offer alternative variations and different packages. These companies also set you up with your first week of stuff to do, such as your first week in the hostel, and activities, like we had a harbour boat cruise which was incredible, city walk, and they also took you to a place called base camp just outside the city which was really cool and we went hiking, sand boarding plus did loads of other cool activities. I did have an amazing week and met some really great people. That is one of the best things about it, the meeting of new people when you first get there, or first land in the airport you are guaranteed to have a group of people your going to meet and do all of these cool activities with, and a few of the people from my group I re-met up with such as I met a group of them at Christmas, and I did part of my farm work with someone I met on this trip and I also met a friend in Melbourne who I first met on this trip. So that is one fantastic benefit of doing an intro package. It is basically there to stop you worrying as you know you're going to have an incredible first week in Australia.

The only downside to it is the cost, it is extremely expensive for what it actually is costing around £550 for seven days. Considering a lot of the activities are actually free such as the city walk and the Bondi to Coogee coastal walk. You can also sort a lot of necessities out yourself as mentioned before like bank account, TFN, phone number etc. But I wouldn't have changed it. I am very glad I did it just for the people I met and the amazing time I had even though it was quite expensive. They are also always there for support, if you ever have a question you can just email them and they will get back to you very fast. I think it's also just knowing you have your first week in Australia planned out and sorted, it makes you feel a lot more comfortable and relaxed knowing everything is sorted out for you when you land and saves you stressing out or worrying that you've forgot something. I have put some links below for some of the introduction packages offered so you can have more of a look into it and see if you think it is worth it and what they offer in a bit more detail.

Australia Introduction Package website links:
UltimateOZ (The one I did)- http://www.ultimate.travel/ultimateoz-sydney/
Ozintro- https://www.ozintro.com/
STA Travel- http://www.statravel.co.uk/australia-working-packages.htm

As I say they do range in prices, but they also range in what they offer and the things they sort out for you. So if you do plan on doing an introduction package make sure, you compare them all and see which one suits you best, as said before they have their advantages and disadvantages, as in you can sort a lot of it out yourself really easily, but you will have an amazing first week in Australia that you'll never forget and your guaranteed to make some great mates that you'll probably continue to travel with.

# Costs and Shopping

## Chapter 21-Average Costs Breakdown

This part of the book is going to go through the average costs of everything you may need to purchase when in Australia. This is just a rough average, there are obviously going to be more expensive items and cheaper items if you can find them. This is just to give you a rough idea of what it costs to live and travel and a rough idea of what you will be spending when living in Australia.

Food:
Weekly- $50, this is what I spent in an average week on food shopping when living in Sydney, but it will vary greatly depending on how you eat.
Eggs (12)- $3
Milk 1 Litre- $1
Bread Loaf- $1
1kg Chicken Breasts- $8
Beef Round 1kg- $15
Rice 1kg- $1.50
Cheese 1kg- $10
Potatoes 1kg- $4
Tomatoes 1kg- $5
Bananas 1kg- $3.20
Pasta 1kg- $2
Onions 1kg- $5
24 Sausages- $5
1kg Mince- $5
Pasta/Curry Sauces- $1.50

Drinking (from Supermarket):

Bottle of Water 1.5L- $1.50

Pepsi 1L- $1

Wine 5L- $12

Domestic Beer (6 Pack)- $15

Imported Beer (6 Pack)- $20

Juice 1L- $2

Vodka 1L- $35

Restaurants/Cafés:

Meal Inexpensive Restaurant- $15

Meal Mid Range Restaurant- $25-$50

Meal at McDonald's- $10

Coffee- $4

Dominoes Pizza Takeaway- $5

Subway 6Inch Sub- $5

Drinking/Going Out (In bar or Nightclub)-

Bottle of Beer- $5-$10

Jug of Beer- $20

Spirit and Mixer- $6-$10

Glass of Wine- $5

Bottle of Wine- $20

Nightclub Entry- $10

Transportation: I spent $20 a week if not using Taxis and just using the train.

Return Train Fare 30 mins- $5

Return Bus Fare 1 hour- $4

Monthly Pass- $130

Average Taxi Fare 30 mins- $40

Clothing:

Pair of Nike Trainers- $130

Flip Flops- $5

Cheap T-shirt- $5

Cheap Shorts/Swim Trunks- $10

Branded Summer Dress (H&M)- $100

Pair of Leather Shoes- $120

Branded Sweater/Jacket (Top man)- $60

Leisure and Sports:

Gym Membership 1 month- $60

Cinema Ticket- $18

Swimming Pool- $10

Tennis Court Rent 1 Hour Weekend- $20

So that is a rough costs of things you might spend while living and working in a city in Australia and the things you may want to buy or be doing. This is just a rough idea on what you might be spending and just allows you to make a bit of a comparison to your home country and possibly plan how much you'll need to save. This next part below will look at what it costs to travel in Australia and the average cost to do trips and go and see things. More information on the cost of trips will be in chapter 7.

Trips:

Complete East Coast trip including all of your transport from either Sydney to Cairns or Cairns to Sydney, all of your hostels for a month and trips such as kayaking, Whitsunday islands, Fraser island, Snorkelling on the Great Barrier Reef, Surfing, will cost you around $3000.

Sydney Bridge Climb- $140

Sydney Zoo- $50

Snorkelling Great Barrier Reef Day Trip- $100

Diving Great Barrier Reef Day Trip- $250

Ayers Rock Trip 3 nights (not including flights)- $300

1 Hour Surf Lesson Bondi Beach- $70

Surf Board Rent 1 day Bondi Beach- $30

Fraser Island 2 Nights Trip- $400

Whitsunday Islands Trip 2 Nights- $500

Great Ocean Road Week Road Trip- $1000

## Chapter 22-Shopping

When it comes to shopping in Australia there is a lot of choice, just as there is in any other country. There are loads of places to choose from, some more expensive and some cheaper budget places.

When food/grocery Shopping there are a few places you might want to pick from the main three places are Coles, Woolworths and Aldi. All of which are your main supermarkets and sell clothes, electronics etc. They are basically your equivalents of Tesco or Asda in the UK. One thing to mention is that supermarkets don't sell alcohol in Australia. Supermarkets are not allowed to sell alcohol in store, often there are stores attached to the side called bottle shops and these sell any alcohol you may need, there is usually one close to the main supermarket. Another option for your grocery’s is the local markets which are often cheaper than supermarkets for vegetables and fruits. The market in China town in Sydney is cheap and then in Melbourne there is the Queen Victoria Market, both of which are very big and offer a range of options. In Sydney for example you can get 3 bags of fruit or vegetables for $5 which is great value compared to the same products you would buy in a supermarket.

*(Queen Victoria Market, Melbourne)*

When it comes to clothes shopping again there are hundreds of different shops and choices from your branded shops to your cheaper alternatives. They have all your usual shops such as Nike, Topman, H&M and many others. In Australia Branded clothing tends to be a bit more expensive than in Europe but there is loads of choice and you will see all of this when just walking down the high-street. For cheaper options when it comes to clothing you have K-mart which I found to be the cheapest place and also offer reasonable quality. This is great if you need a pair of flip flops which you can pick up for $3 or some swimming trunks for $10 they also sell all of your other bits like electronics, toys, home-ware items such as pillows, blankets, lights etc. So if your moving into a new apartment and not wanting to spend to much on furnishing it K-Mart is probably the best place to start as it's cheap and has a lot of choice. There are also other department type stores like Myer which sells a range of things, it's kind of like a more expensive version of K-mart, basically being a home-ware store, they also sell clothes etc.

If your wanting to eat out in Australia or get a takeaway it's actually reasonably priced when compared to Europe, you can often go and get a pub meal and a beer for under $15 which is great when your looking at around $5 for a beer anyway. There are obviously more expensive fancy places which you might want to treat yourself to, like have brunch around Sydney harbour, which is obviously going to cost you more but well worth it for the view. When it comes to fast food Australia is also pretty cheap, Mcdonalds and KFC are around $10 for a meal which is about the same as Europe equalling around 6-7 pound. You can get a medium pizza in dominoes for $5 and a range of toppings which is fantastic value and super cheap. Places like subway are also really cheap being only $5 for a 5 inch sub and $8 for a foot long. There are also other places that are pretty cheap, like sushi shops or random sandwich shops. Most of them offering a meal with a drink for under $10, a lot of places you can pick up just food for under $5. Another great little shop is 7/11 and you will find these everywhere, literally every street corner. These very useful, they sell most things you could need such as phone top-ups, lottery tickets, food, drinks, coffee, cakes and even hot food. It's basically like a commercial corner shop. One thing I used them often for is coffee, you can get a cup of coffee for $1 here which is super cheap, it doesn't taste too bad either.

If you need to buy any other bits such as maybe fancy buying a skateboard, surfboard, car, bicycle etc. Check out www.gumtree.com.au/ there will be loads of other backpackers selling these kinds of things and they will usually be so much cheaper than buying them brand new in a shop. So definitely use Gumtree to your advantage and have a look on there for stuff you need to buy, even things like sofas or computers. If your shopping for Electronics in Australia such as need to buy a new phone or Laptop, I would definitely do your research online finding out what deals there are rather than going into a shop, it's probably going to be a lot cheaper and you will have a better chance of getting a good deal and can compare different products, but again there are shops that sell stuff like this such as Apple stores and phone provider shops.

## Chapter 23-Where to Party? And Drinking

In this Section I am only going to talk about places to Party in the main cities as I obviously didn't go everywhere, but I will mention about the best places to go and which nights and how much the drinks and entry in each of these places is. One thing I did find is that drinking out in Australia is pretty expensive, you can soon see yourself flying through $100 on a night out so I would definitely recommend drinking before you go out, if you're in a hostel this is going to happen anyway, you probably won't even need to buy any drinks out which is what we often did or just one or two which isn't going to break your bank balance. Also with the hostels they often take you out to specific clubs on certain nights, so just go with the flow and follow everyone else, you often get a free drink in these places or reduced entry costs anyway which is great. When drinking in Australia the best places to pre drink before you go out are often the hostels, even if your not staying in a hostel you should try and get to one of your mates hostels, as these allow for a fantastic atmosphere, loads of new people to hang out with and they're always great fun.

You've probably also heard of goon, if you haven't you will come across it when living in Australia. It's basically boxed wine and it's ridiculously cheap. You will probably come across it as soon as you get into a hostel in Australia. It usually costs around $10 for 5 litres and we often used to just go halves so $5 on a box of goon and we'd be pretty drunk. There are loads of different types of goon like red, dry white, but the most common and best tasting is fruity lexia its got a more fruity taste, you can mix it with juice if you want, or some sort of soda makes it taste much better as I'm sure you can imagine from the cost of the stuff, it doesn’t taste great at all. Then again you could just get beers but it's probably going to cost you rather than $5 more like $30 to get drunk.

These are not all of the clubs/bars in each city there are going to be a lot more but these are just the most well known ones particularly for backpackers and the places where most people go.

Sydney: Sydney does have Lockout laws at 1am, this means if you leave the club after 1am you won't be able to get back in and this goes for any club in NSW. Also to take note clubs cannot serve doubles.

Scu Bar- This is located right on the corner near central and can get very busy, it is usually free but they may charge you $5 if it's busy. Monday night is the busiest night, if you arrive around 12 you will be waiting for a while to get in. It is a pretty small club but has some great nights and is usually a lively backpacker environment. 3pm-3am 7 days.

Side Bar- Like Scu Bar, this is located in the centre just around the corner. It's located underneath Wake Up hostel. Again its busiest night is Monday night so a lot of backpackers swap between the two, but it also gets very busy on Friday and Saturdays. I prefer Scu Bar, I never really liked side bar myself, but I know a lot of people that did, and I did have some great nights there. Like Scu Bar it can get very busy and you might be waiting in line a long time so your best bet is to get there early and get a stamp. 4pm-3am 7 days.

Home- This is the Biggest Nightclub in Sydney and infact Australia, it has 3 floors and about 7 different rooms all playing different kinds of music. I spent a lot of Saturday nights here. It can be very expensive to get in I think around $20 on some nights, but we used to get in for $5 as the hostel had a deal, you often see people selling $5 tickets on the street which are usually legitimate. It's also really cool as it's situated on darling harbour and there is a big glass window so you can party with a view.

Chinese Laundry- This is less off your typical chart scene and more house, electronic and drum and bass music. It usually costs around $10 to get in, and does get really busy later on, so if you want to avoid the lines, definitely get there a bit earlier. It's not really a well know backpackers scene but still good to party, especially if your living in Sydney.

Ivy- This is more of an upper class establishment, located much a bit further up George street. It's usually quite expensive, especially on Friday and Saturday nights, but it is free on Thursdays, which is great as it means a lot more backpackers are going, it can be very busy, so it's best to get there a bit earlier, especially if you are going on a Thursday as I'm sure you can imagine how busy it can get being the only free night of the week.

Melbourne: Melbourne has lockout laws from 2 am, so the same as above if you leave the club after 2am you will not be allowed back in.

Revolver- A very popular club located in the heart of Melbourne. It has a very good reputation and always gets very very busy. It has a 24 hour license so can run all night which is probably where it gets a lot of its reputation from. It plays a range of music from live bands, Hip Hop, Dance and Rock. But it's definitely a place you have to go if your in Melbourne.

The Joint Backpackers Bar- This is one of the most famous backpacker bars in the city and is busy most nights of the week. It is set right next to Flinders street station so has a very central location, is great for meeting other backpackers.

Therapy Nightclub- Another reasonably sized nightclub located on Southbank not far from Flinders street station. Has 2 bars and plays a range of music.

Co Nightclub- Also located on Southbank, they play usually commercial dance music and R&B this is only a small venue and can only hold up to around 150 people.

There are loads more bars and clubs in Melbourne, some that I would've never heard of located in quirky little places or down some backstreet's it's all about finding them. These are just the few I heard of to party while I was there for 5 days.

Cairns: Cairns again has a 1 am lockout law and this is the same for any bar in Queensland.

Gilligan's- This is attached to Gilligan's backpackers resort and is the largest place to party in Cairn's. It's popular with locals and travellers and is usually busy every night as it's free entry for everyone staying in Gilligan's, so most people staying there go there or at least end up there later on in the night. They play a range of music from Hip Hop, R&B, house and dance. If you are not staying in the hostel entry usually costs around $5 which isn't too bad at all. There is a large outside area with benches and seating and also some pool tables, and then a big dance area inside.

The Woolshed- Probably the second most popular place to party in Cairns, it is always usually very lively and has very good offers on drinks. It's often free to get in as people hand out wristbands on the streets all day and you often get given them when walking back from the lagoon or through town, otherwise it's usually around $5. It's a good little venue with a dance floor, lots of seating areas and an outside area. It's pretty cool to as you can dance on the tables. These are the two main places, we often used to start the night in The Woolshed as it is free before 11pm, and then head over to Gilligan's at about 1pm.

These are probably the two main places you will go to party in cairns, there are other bars and pubs which you might go to and places such as the casino, but they are the two spots where backpackers tend to go. They also have a party bus in cairns where it takes you around all the local bars and clubs with free entry and often some free drinks, this does have an upfront cost, but usually there will be quite a few people doing it, so could be quite fun.

There are loads more clubs and bars in each of these cities and I'm sure you will find them out yourself, but these are just the few that I heard of and the good ones I experienced. When going out in Australia they can be a lot stricter than in Europe, so make sure you have your ID and if you are really drunk when you turn up to a club, more often than not they won't let you in. Also I didn't mention places to party when travelling up the east coast of Australia, this is because there are only 1-2 places in each place you stop and you'll end up just following the crowd and going with whoever your with, you'll always find somewhere and always have a good time.

## Chapter 24-Budgeting Your Money

Budgeting? A word a lot of people hate the thought of. But unfortunately if your wanting to travel Australia, maybe further and make the most of your trip your going to have budget your money. I'm not saying that you have to save it all and not spend anything because of course you want to have an amazing time but it is very important in a number of ways. Number one when working in Australia your going to be wanting to save some of your money for you big trips or wherever you plan on going, number 2 when doing the trips your going to have to budget for each day to be sure you don't spend it all and have none left and still have a week of travelling left to do, because you can be sure without any money your not going to enjoy it. And finally number 3 your probably going to want some money left over for when you finish your travels, this is always a good idea as then it gives you some time and leeway to decide what you want to do next and will just make you feel much more comfortable about arriving home.

It's hard to plan budgeting as everyone has there own routes and goals of what they want to achieve when travelling but this is just a rough guide that should help you, or at least give you an idea of how to budget your own finances. If you plan on working in Australia before or after your travels your probably going to want to save some money while you do it, especially as the pay is so good in Australia. I worked in Australia first, I did go to Australia with some money and went to Sydney to work and stayed there for 4 months working in a call centre and managed to save a fair amount of money. When you do manage to find yourself a job for the long term (meaning 2-8 months) in whichever city you are living here's a list of the things you should do which will help save for your travels:

1. Find out how much your job is going to earn you roughly per week, this way you know exactly how much money is coming in and what you

have to use.

2. Take your rent/accommodation costs of this and then see how much you are left with.
3. Work out how much you spend on food each week, like general grocery shopping for me this was $50 a week.
4. Work out how much you are going to spend on other things, or other expenses you are going to have such as phone contract, haircut, transport, drinking money, money for going out places at the weekend. For me this was $70.
5. So that works out at $120 a week which I can spend.
6. Now every week, what I used to do would be whenever I would spend something I would write it down just in the notes of my phone what it was and the cost and keep a total and make sure I wouldn't spend over $120.
7. Then you can take your expenses of your weekly pay, I would say $150 a week just to be careful and then you are always going to save more than you think if you stick to $120, and in case of emergency's such as you have to buy a new phone etc. Always take of more than what you plan to spend a week. And take your accommodation costs of.
8. Then this will leave you with an amount you should save every week, from this you can work out how much you should save in a month, 3 months etc. And then you can plan what travels you can do with these savings.
9. Then every week when you get paid transfer your weekly spending money into your account and put all the rest in your savings.

This may all sound a bit extreme, but it will literally take you a few minutes each week just to note down what you spend and is going to make your travels much more enjoyable as you won't have to be worrying about money and can plan all your travels knowing how much you are going to save.

Another time your going to have to budget your money is when your actually doing the travelling. This is much easier as your just going to be spending. This is very important probably more important than the actual saving because if you don't budget properly and run out of money part way through your trip, you don't really want to be calling mum and dad asking them for money or a flight ticket home, completely ruining this awesome trip you probably worked hard to save for. There’s a few tips I have to make sure this doesn’t happen. First work out how long you are going to be travelling for and how much you are likely to spend each day, food, alcohol, activities, transport, accommodation. If you have booked your east coast trip for example it is likely that your transport, accommodation and activities are already included so you only need to account for food and alcohol and a few other bits. Once you've worked out how much you are going to be spending each day, multiply that by the total number of days travelling, I always add a couple days on just to be safe and leave me with some spare. This will give you a total amount that you will need for the trip, it's best to do this before so you know how much you need to save. Another tip is I would always have backup money say $200-$300 for the whole trip just in case you need it, as you never know you might be travelling and everyone decides to do something or you see a great deal, and if you didn’t have that back up money you would have never been able to do it. A good example is when I was in Thailand I found out it was the cheapest place in the world to complete my open water dive course and it was something I really wanted to do, luckily I had that backup money so I could do it even though it wasn't originally in my budget, I had that spare money there just in case something like that did pop up.

Other ways to help with you budgeting is set yourself some targets like say you want to save $1000 by the end of the month, make sure it's something reasonable but not something to easy, this will keep you motivated and on track to saving. Another way of keeping motivated to save is keep planning your trip while your saving, look at photos of where your going and don't forget what your actually saving for, plan those trips like a skydive or diving this will remind you that all that saving is going to be well worth it.

These are just some rough ideas or ways of budgeting your money, this is the way I did it and found it worked fantastically for me. Everyone has their own ways of budgeting and saving, you might find that this just wouldn't work for you, or it might work really effectively as it did for me. It doesn't have to be as extensive as what I showed above, but my advice would be definitely keep a rough idea of what your spending and have coming in.

# Transportation

## Chapter 25- Local/Public Transport

Public transport in each city varies, I am just going to talk about Sydney and Melbourne as these are the two most popular cities to live in and the two I experienced public transport in. I found the public transport in Australia to be great, it is usually reliable, fast and reasonably priced especially when compared to the cost of London's transport.

Sydney- When living or even travelling in Sydney I would highly recommend you to get an Opal card. I am not sure on the exact price of individual fares but they are about $5 return for a 30 minute each way trip. With an Opal card it charges you at a reduced price, and after your first 8 trips each week it is free, which is in my opinion fantastic. Like me if you work 5 days a week by Friday all your trips after are free which means you can travel anywhere you want on the weekend for free for as long as you like. I used to travel for about 30 minutes to work and home and I would just top up my opal $20 a week. Also with an Opal card on Sundays your journey is capped at $2.50 max, so if you haven't used your 8 journeys that week, it will cost you no more than $2.50 a journey, so for example you could get the ferry to manly for $2.50. You can top your Opal card up online or in most convenient stores like 7/11 but will usually find you can't do it in train stations unless there is a shop in there. You can also get to the airport for $10 each way using your opal card.

*(View of the Harbour Bridge from Sydney's Train, Milsons Point)*

Some great places to go using the opal card especially if it is free after your 8 trips or on a Sunday, are manly beach you can take the ferry, the blue mountains which takes around 2 hours on the train, the royal national park which is about an hour and a half, that's just to name a few. You can also get to the majority of the local beaches using public transport. There are trains going all over Sydney, and you can get buses to smaller places, such as certain beaches where trains do not go such as Coogee beach and Maroubra beach. You can also take surfboards and bicycles on public transport as you will see a lot of people doing.

Another option of public transport in Sydney is taxi's, Sydney's trains and buses do stop at night, most trains stop before midnight and sometimes your only option for getting home may be a taxi. They are pretty expensive just the same as anywhere but if you split the cost between 3-4 of you then it's not to bad at all, a 30 minute journey will probably cost you around $50 altogether.

Melbourne: Melbourne like Sydney has its own version of the Opal card, it's called a Myki Card. Again as with the opal you simply top up the card at local convenience stores, and tap on and tap off when you leave. It can be used on trains, trams and buses and I would highly recommend getting one, as it'll end up saving you a lot of money rather than buying single tickets. A Myki card does cost $6 to start with though. Myki works in zones, so it will cost you so much depending on which zone you go in, for example you can get a week pass for zone 1 and 2 for $37. As you will probably know about Melbourne the centre has a massive tram network, which runs through the city, this is great as you can hop on and hop of the trams when you need, they run regularly and stop often. Also introduced in January 2015, is the free tram zone in Melbourne CBD, which makes it much easier for tourists and commuters to get around the city. It stops at major locations like Flinders Street, Spring Street and La Trobe Street. It also stops along Elizabeth Street and the docklands area. This is great if you are just visiting Melbourne as a tourist as will save you loads on public transport. The train and tram services in Melbourne runs between 5am and midnight and on Sundays 7am to 11pm.

Again another option in Melbourne is using taxis but these are a lot more expensive than public transport especially if travelling long distances. Costing around $40 for a 30 minute trip, but it may be your only way of getting home after a night out, so the choice is there.

The best option if you want to go from the Airport to the city is by using the Sky Bus, this departs right outside the airport, and is $18 each way or $30 return. It is about a 30 minute trip and will drop you off at southern cross station, from there it's a little walk into the city about 15 minutes or you could get a train/tram. You can get a public bus using your Myki card it will cost you about $8 each way but takes like an hour and a half. Then your final option again is a taxi, costing you about $55 to the city but if there is 3-4 of you it's actually cheaper than going on the Sky Bus.

## Chapter 26-Buses Around Australia

There are quite a few options when it comes to getting a bus around Australia. Most of the buses cover all of the most populated areas and go up and down the coasts and to some places more inland. They range in prices and how often they leave. Buses do take a long time, you need to remember Australia is a huge country so getting from one place to another that may look close on a map, may infact be a 12 hour bus trip away, but buses are one of the easiest and cheapest ways of getting around Australia.

East Coast:
There are two main choices when picking your bus for the east coast, The Greyhound, or The Premier Bus. The more popular one is the greyhound bus but they both go to very similar places, especially up and down the East Coast.

The Greyhound

These buses are very comfortable, they even offer USB charging ports and free Wifi, even though often it's very slow and will take hours to load a page, but sometimes it works fast, it's entirely luck. The greyhound probably has one of the most extensive bus networks in Australia as covers a vast area, here are the main places it stops, it does stop at smaller locations but you can view them on the website on the network map:

- Sydney
- Brisbane
- Cairns
- Adelaide
- Melbourne
- Darwin
- Alice Springs
- Surfers Paradise
- Byron Bay

Also stopping at a lot of places inbetween, as you can see it stops at a lot of places so gives you a lot of options. There are also a lot of options in regards to passes and buying tickets:

- KM Passes- This is where you get a pass for a certain amount of kilometres 1000, 2000, 5000 and 10,000 and you can travel wherever you like.
- Short Hop Passes- Allow you to hop between two close destinations and you can stop at any place inbetween.
- Hop on Hop off Passes- A pass for longer distances so you can get off at any locations you like inbetween those two destinations, for example Sydney and Cairns for your east coast trip, getting on and off where you

like on the way.

The passes range in price depending on where it is you are wanting to go but they are reasonably priced for what they offer and the distances they let you go. From Sydney to Cairns it would cost you $430. Or from Sydney to Melbourne it would cost $100. Which is more than reasonable. They also run fairly often up the coast on average 3 buses each day so you have a range of times to pick from. More information can be found on there website. www.greyhound.com.au/

Premier Travel Service

This is a less popular service as is not as well known, it is quite a lot cheaper than the greyhound but it does not offer free Wifi or USB charging ports. The bus only runs up the East coast so from Melbourne to Cairns stopping at all your main locations and the little locations inbetween so:

- Melbourne
- Sydney
- Brisbane
- Gold Coast
- Surfers Paradise
- Cairns

So this is a good option if you are doing your East coast trip the cost of the different passes vary so from Sydney to Cairns it is only $295 which is over $100 cheaper than the greyhound. This is who we chose to do our east coast with, and we found it to be great, it was just like normal bus but just cost a lot less than the greyhound, they stop at all the locations you need up the east coast. We often found them to be a lot quieter too as most people choose the greyhound which means on those overnight buses you can layout to sleep. The other difference between the two is that this only has one bus going up the coast each day which means you don't really have a choice of times of when you leave, which for us was fine as it didn't really matter when we got there, but for some it may be important. You can get more information on there website www.premierms.com.au/newhome/home.asp.

West Coast:
These are the main buses that go up and down the west coast. Not as many people travel the west coast, and it's a lot less popular with backpackers so there are not as many options in regards to travel passes even though they are available.

Trans WA
Trans WA is a bus company that covers most of SW Australia stopping at over 240 destinations. The most north they go is as far as Kalbarri and then they go right down south to Albany and Esperance as well as Perth and Perth Airport. So they have great transport links and connections and go reasonably far inland too. Just as a rough idea to costs from Perth to Albany which is about 5 hours will cost $80 for an Adult. There is more information on the website www.transwa.wa.gov.au/.

Southwest Coach lines
This is another bus company that offers buses in the south west of Australia, I used this company to travel from Perth to Margaret River and back when completing my farm work, I found them to have good coaches that were reasonably comfortable however when I was waiting at Perth airport the bus was about 30 minutes late, which did cause me to panic and think I was in the wrong place. Again the buses go to a variety of places throughout the south west of Australia sticking to six major routes, not as many as Trans WA. Just as a rough idea of prices, to travel from Perth Airport to Margaret River will cost you

around $65 and again this journey is around 5 hours. Again more information is available on the website www.southwestcoachlines.com.au/.

Integrity Coaches
This is a bus company that operates buses in the north west of Australia. So they run from Perth all the way up to Broome. They stop at a range of places the major ones being, Perth, Exmouth, Coral Bay, Broome, Karijini national park among others. They do offer more than just basic return and one way tickets as the south west buses do, they offer hop on hop off passes. You can get a pass from Perth to Broome for $365, this is only valid one way and is valid for up to 12 months, allowing you to stop anywhere you want inbetween. So this is a fantastic option if you want to explore the more quite north west Australia. More information is again available on the website www.integritycoachlines.com.au.

These are the main buses that you will most likely want to use during your time in Australia while travelling. There are hundreds of others that run more locally and specific buses that run to more rural places, like if you were doing your farm work. I just explained the main ones that you will come across and use, if you do need more specific buses or buses for other regions just give Google a search of where you want to go to and from and I'm sure it will come up with various options and any other information you may need.

## Chapter 27-Trains Around Australia

When it comes to getting around Australia by train there is a very extensive network that runs throughout the country I will go through the main ones below explaining costs, what they include, where they go and basic prices. The trains in this section are just going to be long national trips throughout Australia inbetween regions. Regional trains run the same as the public trains, so you will be able to buy tickets in a station or even online. I never used any regional trains as they tend to be more expensive than buses, so I just stuck to using the buses, but they are a lot quicker, more comfortable and often offer some incredible scenic views which cannot be offered by any other form of transport.

The Ghan:
This is a train that runs from Darwin to Adelaide, through Alice Springs and the red centre. This train journey looks really amazing passing through the centre of the Australian outback stopping at all the main places. The distance is just under 3000 kilometres and takes 54 hours. For a backpacker for a single cabin on the Ghan travelling from Adelaide to Darwin it will cost you around $1900.

The Indian Pacific:
This train runs from Perth to Adelaide to Sydney. Stopping at a few places inbetween and is a huge 4352 kilometre trip. For the whole trip for a backpacker from Sydney to Perth it will costs you around $2200, again you can stop of inbetween.

The Overlander:
This Train runs from Melbourne to Adelaide so is a much shorter Journey of only 828 kilometres. Once again with amazing scenery and the trains being really comfortable. There are also a number of stops between the two start and finish destinations. This train will cost around $80 for a one way ticket.

The XPT:
This train runs from Melbourne to Sydney to Brisbane, those being the three main spots. Also stopping of at smaller places and offering alternative destinations. To travel from Melbourne to Brisbane on an overnight train will cost you around $180 again offering great views that may not be seen by plane

or bus.

That's all I can mention about the major long journey trains in Australia, there are many smaller local trains such as ones specific to Queensland and various passes available such as the discovery pass which allows you unlimited travel for a certain period of time being it 1, 3, 6 or 12 months, but only on selected trains. There are lots of options if getting a train is your thing and you have a large budget. They may definitely be worth checking out for an incredible experience. There is loads more information about all of the trains available, booking, costs and anything else you might need to know is on this website www.railaustralia.com.au/index.php.

## Chapter 28-Domestic Flying in Australia

Flying domestically in Australia is really easy, probably about as easy as getting a bus or train anywhere. You only have to turn up at the airport about 2 hours before your flight and just the same as a normal flight, you check in and drop your bags, go through security and your done. You then just get your flight, pick up your bags and don't even have to go through security in the place you land. When you are flying throughout Australia, make sure you tell whoever is taking you, to take you to the domestic airport and not the international one. For example, if you're getting in a taxi as they are usually two different airports, they will usually ask you, but you don't want to end up at the wrong airport. With domestic flying you can also check in online up to 24 hours before your flight and if you are travelling with hand luggage only then this is great, as you can check in online then print of your boarding passes at one of the machines in the airport, you don't even need to queue up for check in. Even if you have bags you can still do this, the airlines usually have two separate lines one for people checking in and one for people just dropping their bags off.

There are three main domestic airlines that run throughout Australia, and they vary in price, but also vary in service and comfortableness. It would entirely depend on your budget, and sometimes if it's a reasonably long flight say from Sydney to Perth or Sydney to Cairns it may be worth paying an extra $20 to go with the better Airline. The three main Airlines are Tiger Air, JetStar and Virgin Australia, the two budget airlines are Tiger Air and JetStar. I have flown with all three and can say they all greatly range in how comfortable they are. JetStar usually offer the cheapest flights and the seats are okay, you don't get a great amount of room, and there's not much service. But if it's just a short flight and your on a budget they're okay, much the same for Tiger Airways. They're not the most comfortable planes in the world but if it's just a little 2 hour flight then they are all right. I have flown with them both a number of times as they are usually a lot cheaper than virgin. Virgin Australia are a lot more luxury and if the flight difference is only $20 and it's a long flight I would definitely recommenced paying the extra. The seats are a lot more comfortable and on the long flights such as when I flew from Sydney to Perth which is about 4 hours, they give you food, and constant drinks, you also get in-flight entertainment, whereas on the same flight with JetStar I got none of this. The difference can make your flight a lot more enjoyable, but this is why Virgin Australia are usually a lot more expensive.

Domestic flying is usually reasonably priced if you find a good deal or book early enough, and it's probably the best way to get around Australia with it being such a big country. Here's a rough idea of what it may cost to fly between certain places, it will vary depending on the season, or if it's during school holidays but it's a good guideline. Try to book your flights in advance, the best is from 6-8 weeks as they will be a lot cheaper. This prices below are when booking 6 weeks in advance.

Sydney to Melbourne- $70 (JetStar) 1.5 Hours
Sydney to Cairns- $130 (Tiger Air) 3 Hours
Sydney to Perth- $200 (Tiger Air) 5 Hours
Melbourne to Cairns- $150 (Tiger Air) 3.5 Hours
Sydney to Brisbane-$70 (Tiger Air) 1.5 Hours
Sydney to Ayers Rock- $230 (Jet Star) 3.5 Hours
Sydney to Gold Coast- $100 (Tiger Air) 1.5 Hours
Sydney to Hobart, Tasmania- $150 (Jet Star) 2 Hours

As you can see it is pretty cheap to get around Australia by air, it is also the fastest option so you'll probably use it a lot if you're planning on doing a lot of travelling around Australia. Another thing to note when domestic flying there is no quarantine like when first entering Australia, it's a lot quicker especially when landing and getting of the plane you can be from the plane to outside within 10 minutes if your luggage is near the front.

## Chapter 29-Buying a Car/Van

Another option when you're planning on travelling, or even just for where you are living so you can go on little adventures, is buying a car or some sort of camper van. Sometimes it is a lot easier to hop on the bus, but having a car allows you to explore vast, less touristy, unpopular places and really gives you the freedom to go exactly where you want. This is relatively easy when in Australia and there are loads of options. There are some things you need to make sure the car has to make sure it is road worthy and most of all legal before you drive it on the roads though. You are obviously also going to need a driving license to be able to drive in Australia.  If you are buying a car from another backpacker, or from somewhere like gumtree you can get something called a

REVS check, this will check to see whether the seller has the rights to sell the vehicle so basically confirms it's not stolen.

When you finally buy your car or van, after you pay the seller, you will be given a slip which you need to take to the local Motor Vehicle Registry (MVR). The slip is used to transfer the ownership of the car, it includes the car details, the seller details and the new owner details. If the registration is due, you will pay for your registration at the same time and get your service done if required. At the MVR they will then give you the documents that say the car has been registered in your name. You need to keep this document as when you sell the car the same process will need to be completed but with you being the seller.

Costs:

When buying a car there are obvious costs that will be associated with it. For you to be able to legally drive the car, just as there is in any other country. Just for reference Rego is what the Australians call registration.

- The registration transfer fee, this is currently $24 in NSW you only have to pay this if the car already has a Rego.
- When in Australia you will have to get a Rego for you car or van if it does not have it, if the car does have it it will usually be advertised as 3 months Rego left etc. It is a legal requirement, which is basically registration and is one of the only costs associated with buying a car in Australia. Included in this comes basic compulsory third party insurance which is required by law. No other insurance is needed but you can get some which covers you from fire, theft etc. But it is not a requirement. Different states do have different laws when registering your vehicle, so it's a lot easier to buy a car from the place you are currently living. Registration costs vary depending on your state, on the car and for how long you need it, you can get a Rego for varying months. You can apply

for your Rego online. Once you get a Rego you will get a sticker to put in your front window, much like a UK tax disk.

- You may also want to buy breakdown cover, this is going to be very important if you are travelling long distances, you don't want to be broken down in the middle of nowhere because that would completely ruin your trip. It's good to have the backup just in-case, once again breakdown cover varies in price dependent on what sort of cover you get and there are loads of different places you can get it from, but I would definitely recommend it if you are planning on doing a lot of travelling.

Basic considerations to take when buying a vehicle:

- Has it had any previous accident damage, if so how good were the repairs.
- Does it have any rust.
- How is the engine condition does it make any odd sounds when it running, is there any smoke coming out of the exhaust this may signify future engine problems.
- Is the water in the radiator clean and oil free.
- Is there any presence of a creamy white substance in the oil, this could mean that water from the cooling system is getting into the oil.
- Let the car stand for a while after it has been running and see if there is any oil dripping from under the engine.
- Is there any windscreen damage, even a small chip can lead to a major crack and extra costs.
- Do the tires have good tread.
- Does the vehicle have a roadworthy certificate (Rego).

Other things you can do to make sure the car is all good and worth buying is get it inspected by a mechanic this may costs you extra initially but could end up saving you major problems when your travelling in it. Always ask if you can have a test drive to make sure it drives well and you actually like driving it.

*(Car one of my mates bought in Sydney, Costing around $600)*

Where to buy your vehicle:

Buying a used car in Australia is pretty easy, there are loads of options and lots of people selling them, you just need to be careful to make sure that the car is okay, and everything is working correctly, so you don't get ripped off. Sometimes you can get some really cheap vans/cars that backpackers have used to travel in, and are in a rush to get rid of. Say they have a flight leaving the country this means that they sometimes sell them ridiculously cheap just to get rid of them because it's better than leaving it. Some of these are great options as they come with all camping gear in, fitted with beds, curtains, cooking equipment, BBQs, surfboards and properly kitted out which is great.

- Gumtree- Gumtree is always a good option they have loads of people selling second hand cars and vans, with a range of prices and types of vehicle. When you find a vehicle you like, you just give them a call and go and inspect. This can be risky, as the vehicles may be damaged but as long as you go and check them out and know what your looking for, or take someone with you that does, you will be fine, and you could end up getting a great deal.
- Backpacker Car Markets- There are a range of backpacker car markets, usually in the bigger cities like Sydney and Melbourne, where backpackers are trying to get rid of their cars as their leaving. It usually works in an auction type of way, but again this is another option and can offer some bargain prices, just make sure to check the vehicles out before buying.
- Hostel Notice Boards- There are always cars and vans being advertised on hostel notice boards with a range of information about them and a phone number, this is usually backpackers that are about to leave the country/city trying to sell their vehicles quick and can sometimes offer some good deals.
- Second Hand Car Dealer- This is another option and is going to be more reliable but also a lot more expensive. Buying them of a dealer is probably going to end up costing you far more than of say Gumtree, but it might be worth going and having a look, seeing what they offer and getting some advice.

The price range of cars does vary greatly, it will usually depend on your location, the condition of the car, whether it has a Rego, and what's included in it. If you are in more remote places like Darwin or quieter towns up the west coast car prices are going to be a bit more expensive, just because there is less available. Whereas if your buying your car in a bigger city like Sydney or Melbourne it's going to be a lot cheaper as there are a lot more backpackers and cars available. In Sydney car/vans range from $1000-$3000, obviously if you are paying $3000 you will be wanting something in a lot better condition. Finally when buying a car, make sure you look around if you know you are going to be travelling in a month, don't rush into it and buy a car. Take your time, have a look around and make sure you don't get ripped off as it could end up costing you a lot of money on repairs, which unfortunately happens to a lot of backpackers. Also give yourself some time to sell the car, it may be difficult if your leaving straight after your trip, but advertise it and make sure everything is up to scratch, you will then hopefully get a lot more back for it, maybe even what you paid for it which would be great.

## Chapter 30-Renting a Car/Van

Renting a Camper van is the alternative to buying a car or van, it can be a lot less stressful and you don't have the whole buying/selling/breakdown and other things to sort and worry about. Hiring a camper van will usually come fitted with the best equipment such as a reasonably comfy bed, stove, pots, pans and all kitted out with curtains etc. It also gives you the freedom to go where you want and stop for as long as you want, and it will save you on accommodation costs.

When renting a Camper van or car in Australia you need to have a driving license, one thing with renting your transport is age. Unfortunately most companies only hire camper vans to people over the age of 25 and cars for people over the age of 21, there are a few hire companies that are different and do rent to younger people such as Travel Wheels, they hire to people between the ages of 18 to 21. The cost of renting is usually a lot higher if you are under 25 and significantly more if you are under 21, also the terms and conditions and deposit are likely to be much greater, so if you don't have a lot of money to spare then this probably isn't an option.

*(Jeep we hired in Airlie Beach, Cost $80 for the day)*

Average Costs Associated with Hiring a Camper van:

- You will have to pay a deposit on the vehicle before you use it, this will get given back to you when you return the vehicle if there is no damage to it, like scratches or bumps etc. Deposit depends on your age and driving experience but can range anywhere from $500 to $2000, also depending on how long you hire the vehicle for.
- You will obviously have to pay to rent the camper van itself, this is

usually done per day, so you pay per day you are going to be using it but I'm sure if your going to be using it for a long time say a month travelling the East coast you could get some sort of deal. Camper van hire can range from $20 a day to over $70 a day but this entirely depends on how many people you are, what kind of camper van you get, what's included, how long you have it for. That being said if you can get a camper van for $30 a day for 2 people that's only $15 each per day for your accommodation and transport, which isn't to bad when hostels can be around $25 themselves a night.

- Fuel, in Australia fuel isn't that expensive, it is relatively cheap, again how much you spend on fuel will depend on the type of vehicle you are driving the bigger obviously the more fuel you are going to use. Currently in Australia (January 2016) fuel is around $1.30 per litre which is rather cheap so fuel won't be a major expense.
- Insurance, you don't need to spend any more on insurance. When you hire a car you will get basic insurance included but if there is any damage to the car. The excess you will have to pay will be quite high, between $500 and $3000 depending on the car/van. You can buy some but it is optional to get additional insurance, this is around an extra $10-$30 a day, again it can be quite expensive but will cover you for any damage, it entirely depends on how you feel about it, and how confident you are driving.
- Breakdown Cover, this is something that I would probably recommend it is usually pretty cheap and maybe you could get a deal but it's usually around $10 extra a day, but covers you if you break down and getting you back on the road again with any minor problems, this can be very useful as Australia is a big country and you don't want to be broken down in the middle of nowhere with no options, it could ruin your trip whereas if you know someone is coming it completely removes the stress and you know

you sorted.

Where to rent:

There are a lot of options when it comes to renting, make sure you look around and find out options and some discount if you hire long term or insurance deals. It depends on your preferences to which one you will pick and what deals you can get. Just have a good look before you commit to one. Here are some links to websites you might want to have a look at, they all offer different types of deals and there are a lot of other options out there, these are just a few of the main ones:

- www.vroomvroomvroom.com.au/campervans/
- www.spaceshipsrentals.com.au/
- www.hippiecamper.com/
- www.wickedcampers.com.au/
- www.motorhomebookers.com/australia/compare_prices.htm?et=Wo9Fw3&et_cid=3&et_lid=14646
- www.jucy.com.au/?_ga=1.129940229.803408325.1448709196

www.mightycampers.com/

- www.thrifty.com.au/

Relocation Deals:

Relocation deals can be a great way to travel Australia for a cheap price. It's basically where other people have hired camper vans and the companies need them somewhere else to rent out. So they offer relocation deals, this is where you get the camper van extremely cheap and often things included like free fuel. You will have to pay a deposit but you will get that back when you drop it off at is designated place. The only downside to this is there is usually a time frame, so a time which you will need to drop it off by which may not give you very long to explore and see the sights. But some do offer longer deals. The locations are often limited so you will have to pick from what is on offer, and it is usually less populated places that the vans are located, although not always. You can often pick up a camper van for $1 a day and $250 free fuel doing these relocation deals, so it's definitely worth looking into if you want cheap transport.

## Chapter 31-Hitch-hiking

Hitch-hiking, although I have not done much of this myself, infact I have only hitch-hiked once and that was from the beach to the city, not a very long distance at all, it took about 30 minutes. Hitch-hiking can be a lot of fun, it gives you the chance to meet loads of new people particularly locals, and you are never really sure of where you are going to be going so can end up in some pretty amazing places, although usually you should try to get someone that is going in a similar direction to you or to somewhere you want to visit. Hitch-hiking has recently had a lot of bad press of people who think it is dangerous, this is having a negative affect as less people are picking up hitch-hikers and less people are hitching themselves. With Hitch-hiking there are a lot of options if you are in a city it's probably best to go to the outskirts and wait for ride there just before a main road and make sure you are standing somewhere where the driver can pull over.

It is not illegal to hitch-hike in Australia but you it is illegal to stand on the side of the road or even the hard shoulder as you could be obstructing traffic. That being said there is no reason why you cannot stand on the grassy areas next to the roads or the footpaths as you will not be obstructing traffic there, it is frowned upon in some states though. It is also questioned whether to use a sign or not with the location of the place you want to go, although it may seem easier, I would probably say it's better not to use a sign maybe just whether you want to go north or south, because then you can ask the driver where they are going and they won't be lying saying their going to the same place as you just to get you in the car.

Tips for getting a ride:
A lot of your rides will probably come from people that have hitched themselves, or from truck drivers that want some company and are bored, to increase your chances make sure you look respectable and non threatening, because looks do matter in these situations and if you look dangerous lets be honest nobody is going to pick you up. I would also smile at the oncoming traffic this way you look more friendly. When a car approaches ask the driver where they are going this way if they seem dodgy or strange it's easy to decline a lift. Also try to travel light, if you have loads of big heavy bags, you are less likely to be picked up as there may be no room and it just looks less appealing, it also means you can travel quicker if you have less bags. Also take a drivers license some people may want to share the driving especially if they are fellow travellers. If you are a female you will get a ride a lot quicker, just because people tend not to see females as dangerous and often feel the need to help out, rather than guys who will probably spend a lot longer waiting.

Safety:
It is really important to make sure you stay safe when hitch-hiking, it is obviously more dangerous than travelling by bus or plane, but it is still safer than other forms of transport such as cycling. The most dangerous thing about hitch-hiking is other cars on the road, and being hit by one, and then the other danger and what everyone thinks happens to every hitch-hiker the chance of getting a bad lift, rarely does this happen although it still occasionally does. It's obviously going to be safer if you travel in a pair, if you travel in more than 2 it is very unlikely you will get a lift as firstly you probably wont all fit in most cars, and secondly it can look intimidating. But pairs is always better than travelling on your own. Another way of making sure your safe is make sure you always have a

mobile phone and more importantly signal, a lot of hitch-hikers will only hitch where there is signal so if it is needed they can call for help or a friend. Don't let the driver put your backpack in the car boot, you can if there is no room, but try to keep your important documents with you, your phone and wallet etc. Also don't feel compelled to accept a lift just because someone has stopped for you. If it doesn't feel right, don't get in. Another ride will come along. Another really obvious point, is don't hitch-hike at night so you can see where your going, and nobody will be able to see you on the side of the road and your are more likely to have an accident.

When waiting for a ride you also want to try and stand somewhere where the car can see you about 500 meters away, not always possible if it's not a long road but this way it allows the driver to slow down and see what your sign says, if your holding one. It's also good for your safety so the cars know your there and can slow down anyway. I would definitely recommend you try hitch-hiking at least once, just so you can experience it, the feeling of never knowing who your going to meet, when someone's going to come, just the overall excitement of it, and it's definitely something I want to try more of in my future travels.

## Places to Visit

This is going to cover some of the best places to visit and things to do while your in Sydney and Melbourne and also what to do when your travelling up or down the East and West Coast, the best places to stop and stuff to do in each of those places. This isn't going to include everything you could possibly do, there will be hundreds of interesting little places to visit that you will find for yourself, and which people will tell you about, it will just cover the main things you can do and some of the less well known stuff that I found from my travels.

## Chapter 32-What to do in Sydney

Sydney is a huge city and there is so much to do here, it would take you years to finish exploring and see everything there is to possibly see, from beaches to hiking, to groovy little suburbs, here's some stuff I would definitely recommend you should do if you get the time while in Sydney.

Must see things if you don't have long:

- Sydney Opera House- A must visit, and an iconic part of Sydney this is probably one of the first things you will do when you get to Sydney is go and see the Opera house, it really is quite incredible.

*(Sydney Opera House and Harbour Bridge)*

- Walk across Sydney Harbour Bridge- The bridge also being another iconic part of Sydney, you can see it from Darling Harbour, but I would recommend walking over it, there are some incredible views of the city.

- Darling Harbour- Another amazing part of Sydney it really is beautiful and a must visit if you don't have long, there are loads of bars and cafés around here you can enjoy, you also have some great views of the city from here. Darling Harbour is great for some afternoon/evening drinks.
- Sydney Royal Botanical Gardens- These are huge botanical gardens right by the ocean, they go all the way round to the Opera house and offer amazing views of the city and harbour. There are also lots of different trees, plants and flower species. I would definitely recommend walking up to Mrs macquarie's chair, it's about a 30 minute walk from the opera house, but offers some of the best views in Sydney overlooking Sydney Harbour, the opera house, the city and the bridge, if you get the chance to go and sit there for sunset it really is beautiful.

*(View of the city from Sydney Botanical Gardens)*

- Bondi- Coogee Walk- This is one of the best walks in Sydney in my opinion make sure you pick a really clear skied day. It's a walk from Bondi beach to Coogee beach and you pass through some smaller beaches beaches on your way like Bronte beach. You could do it in an hour but I would give yourself 2 hours or maybe more, because the views are incredible and you may want to give yourself time to stop and just sit and relax and enjoy the view, also don't forget your swimsuit and a towel because there is plenty of chance for swimming, and if you forget them you'll regret it.

*(View on the Bondi to Coogee Coastal Walk)*

Beaches in Sydney:

As you probably already know there are loads of beaches in Sydney and you will most probably never get to visit them all, some are really popular and easy to get to with public transport, others you will need a car to get too as there is no public transport.

Bondi Beach- The most famous one, and probably the first one you will visit will be Bondi Beach. Public transport runs there from the city and then you can get a bus directly to the beach or it's about a 30 minute walk. The buses are always packed when on your way to Bondi, as it's the most famous beach in Australia, so is likely to be the busiest, but it's honestly amazing when you first see it.

*(A very crowded Bondi Beach)*

Coogee Beach- Another amazing beach, in the eastern suburbs, this one is quite south, and you can get here by the bus, it takes about 45 minutes from the city. This is probably one of my favourite beaches, it's not as big as Bondi, but is amazing if you want to go for BBQs as has a big green park area at the back of the beach with BBQ stoves, where you can play football or chill, it's just a really nice area in general.

Tamarama Beach- This beach is a really small beach, but again it's nice and usually a little bit quieter than Bondi or Coogee. This beach is inbetween Bronte and Bondi. It also has a really nice park area at the back, and often has some cool art shows and stuff going on, again you can get a bus here or just walk from Bondi it will take you about 20 minutes from the city.

Bronte Beach- Bronte beach is inbetween Coogee and Tamarama and again is a pretty small beach, I never really liked it and didn't go often. It's quite a steep beach and again has some green areas at the back with BBQs where it would be nice to go and relax with some food and beers, you can get a bus here which takes about 25 minutes from the city.

Maroubra Beach- Maroubra beach is probably the furthest down the east coast in terms of beaches you can get on public transport, I used to go here a lot to surf, it's a really nice beach and is a lot quieter than all the others and is pretty big, rarely many people out there. There are not as many shops either, but again are some BBQs and bit's of green areas. It does take about an hour on the bus from the city, but worth the trip if you want somewhere quieter to just chill out, the only problem is the last bus back is pretty early about 17.30pm which isn't great.

*(Maroubra Beach)*

Manly Beach- Another amazing beach, one of my favourites with some great memories here. This is north of the city, you can get a bus here but it would take ages, the most popular way to get here is by the ferry, which on a Sunday will only cost you $2.50 with an opal card. This beach is huge, and again a really nice relaxed area, loads of shops and bars around here. There is also a really nice path at the back of the beach, and lots of nice walks around this area too. It's a must visit while you're in Sydney, the ferry also gives you some really amazing views of the harbour.

Hyams beach/Jervis Bay- This is a beach located out of Sydney but it's definitely worth a mention. The only way you can get here is by car, there is no public transport and it's just over a 2 hour drive down the coast to it. The reason it's worth a mention is because its voted the whitest beach in the world, and it really is amazing, if you do have the chance you should go. You should 100% try and make the trip, you could even stay for the weekend and hire a car between a group of you.

*(Hyams Beach, Voted the whitest beach in the world)*

There are loads of other beaches around the Sydney region but those are the mains ones, and specifically ones you can reach by public transport, some that you can't. If you do have a car however there a loads more to choose from such as the northern beaches like freshwater, dee why, curl curl, palm beach just to name a few. And then there are other beaches such as Balmoral beach, and more southern beaches such as Cronulla, so if you do have a car/van it's definitely worth doing some more research as there are some idyllic beaches around the Sydney area.

Hiking/Walking:
There is loads of hiking and walking that you can do in Sydney, with a few national parks in the surrounding area some of them are accessible by public transport. It is definitely worth putting on your hiking boots and doing some exploring, because there are some amazing spots, with waterfalls and swimming

holes, perfect for trips out when you don't fancy the beach.

The Blue Mountains- This is probably the most popular place to visit, as it's easy to get to by public transport. The most popular place a lot of people go is Katoomba, most famously known for the three sisters, three peaks of rock coming out of the side of a mountain, and then Katoomba falls. Katoomba really is beautiful and offers loads of walks and hikes. You can get here on the train, it is a long trip and will end up taking you about 2 and a half hours, so a Sunday is probably best, when you get your $2.50 cap to save you some money. Also offered at Katoomba is the Scenic world attractions, which you can pay for and offers a sky rail over the forest, a trip on the worlds steepest railway, and the cable car. I myself didn't do this, as we didn't feel we had to, we did want to go on the worlds steepest railway, but unfortunately ran out of time. There are loads of shops and cafés at Katoomba, and there are loads of different walks which you can do, it really is beautiful. If you do really enjoy walking and hiking, don't stop there there are so many more amazing places to go hiking in the blue mountains besides Katoomba, do some research depending on what things you like. Just do a search online like, waterfalls in the blue mountains, swimming holes, best views and I am sure you will find something amazing. We did this and found this amazing waterfall and swimming hole with like a mini beach in the middle of the blue mountains just at Linden station. It only took us an hour to get there on the train, but it was quite difficult to find and we had to follow the instructions from the website, no signs were available. Here's just a few places you might want to visit in the blue mountains if you fancy more than Katoomba; Wentworth Falls, Furber Steps, Blue Pool trail, Glenbrook discovery trail.

*(Three Sisters, Blue Mountains, Katoomba)*

Royal National Park- Another not so talked about place, and not often visited by backpackers, but
offers some incredible hikes to swimming holes and waterfalls. The Royal National park is accessible by train, but you will have to look up a walking route before you go, there are loads online. When I looked I just searched walks to waterfalls in the great national park and it came up with loads of routes. Getting there doesn't take to long either about an hour from Sydney central which is pretty good.

*(Swimming Hole in the Royal National Park, Sydney)*

Ku-ring-gai Chase National Park- Another incredible national park, the only difference with this one is unfortunately, you cannot get here by public transport so you will need your own car or van. With a car it will only take you about 40 minutes to get to the start of the national park, it does depend on where you go specifically but it wont take you long at all. Again has some beautiful waterfalls, lakes, rivers, viewpoints and swimming holes. Just search walks with the specific things you want to see into Google and you will get a good range of trail routes.

Sydney Harbour National Park- This is just below Manly beach and you can get here by public transport. It is only a very small national park and it wouldn't take you long to walk around it, but it offers some great views and if your going to manly beach for the day and fancy a bit of a walk it's definitely worth a look.

There are also lots of other walks, not specifically in national parks, but just general walks around the Sydney area which are truly amazing and offer incredible views. Such as getting the train over to North Sydney and having a walk around the area, near Lunar Park and along the harbour from that side, that's just to mention one there are literally hundreds, so definitely have a look online and ask around.

Other things to do in Sydney:
Taronga Zoo- Taronga zoo is another pretty cool place you can visit, it's located just on the shores of Sydney Harbour, in the Mosman district and offers you the chance to see a range of different animals such as Rhinos and Gorillas and also offers some great views of the harbour. It is quite expensive though and costs $45 for one adult to get in, but it is great for a day out.

Lunar Park- Lunar Park is located just on the Harbour in North Sydney, it's like a little carnival but also offers rides, you can recognise it the entrance by the big face, with it's mouth as the entrance. It is free to go in you just have to pay if you want to go on the rides, a ticket to go on all of the rides as much as you want is $48. There are also places you can get food around here, it's also just nice to visit and have a look even if not going on any rides, as offers some great views of the city and the harbour bridge.

*(View from just past Lunar Park)*

Wet n Wild Sydney- If it's a warm day and you have had enough of the beach, then what's better than a water park. Wet n Wild offers a range of water slides, swimming pools, wave pools and lazy rivers to relax in, and makes a great day out. It is pretty expensive being $79 per adult for a day, but you can get some cheaper deals if you wait till the right times, or the end of summer. You can get there by public transport it's not far from Blacktown train station, about 40 minutes by train from Sydney central.

Featherdale Wildlife Park- This place is a great visit especially if your new to Australia. It's not far from the city about 40 minutes on the train to Doonside station and then about a 15 minute walk. It's like a little wildlife park, it's not massively huge like a zoo and has mainly native Australian animals, such as Kangaroos, Penguins, Koalas, Crocodiles, Dingoes and more. They put on feeding times where you can watch them and they give you a talk about them. The best thing about this place is the kangaroos are free roaming so they just go around the park and you can touch them and pet them, and get food to feed them, there are loads of different types of kangaroo and often babies. There is also the chance to pet a koala which is really cute, and it's not very expensive being about $25 for an adult for the day.

*(Selfie with the Kangaroos, Featherdale Wildlife Park)*

Sydney Aquarium- Located just around darling harbour this place is really easy to get to and offers another great day out, for an adult it costs $28 when you buy your tickets online, it is just like any other aquarium and is a great place to visit if it's a rainy day or if there's not much else to do, but if it's a warm summers day I would much rather hit up the beach.

Sydney Tower Eye- This place is definitely worth a visit and often overlooked by backpackers, it's located directly in the city and it will be one of the first things you notice when you get to Sydney. It's the building with the westfields sign on it and definitely stands out being one of the tallest buildings in Sydney. It basically offers 360 views of Sydney from the top which you can walk round and has some amazing views. It only costs about $17 if you book your tickets online, you can also do something called a Sky walk which is where you go outside and walk around the outside with a harness attached but this costs extra (Around $30). You can do this at sunset or night, I did it in the day time and it was really amazing to see Sydney from above.

*(View from Sydney Tower)*

Surfing- If your in Sydney and fancy a go at surfing, what a better place to start, it is quite expensive to hire a surfboard and can get pretty busy but there is a range of places you can do it and  get lessons. The best place in my opinion would be Manly beach as it's a lot bigger, there's a lot more space and it's cheaper than say surfing Bondi Beach, but if you can borrow a surfboard from a friend in a hostel like we did, then we went to Bondi just well, because its Bondi. A surf lesson in Manly for 2 hours will cost you about $70, it is really expensive to learn in Australia, I just bought my own board for $100 and taught myself. To hire will cost you about $20 an hour depending on where you get it from and how close to the beach you hire from, it's best to have a look around or a little look online.

Paddy’s Market/China Town- This is a local market in the china town area, it's just like any other china town in other cities and is pretty small, the market itself offers a range of things from fruit and vegetables, fish, meat and then stuff like souvenirs, clothes etc. Is worth a little visit if you want to buy some gifts or even some cheap food.

Those are the main things you could do in Sydney and would keep you busy for some time. There are loads of other things to do throughout the city which you will hear about from other people, stuff that I have never even heard of doing. If your living in Sydney after doing most of these things you'll probably spend a lot of your days just chilling at the beach and surfing, and exploring finding stuff out for yourself.

## Chapter 33-What to do in Melbourne

Melbourne is the main city in Victoria and the second most popular city to live for backpackers after Sydney. The city is on the coast and has various bars, restaurants and events along the Yarra River. It reminded me of a European city with more little back lanes and cafés and the tram system running through the centre of the city. A great place to chill out and offering free Wifi is the Federation Square, which is right next to Flinders Street Station on the bank of the Yarra River. There is also a giant TV screen often playing sports or the news.

Must see things if you don't have long:

Queen Victoria Market- This is the largest open air market in the southern hemisphere, making it a must visit, they offer everything you could possibly think off and it's definitely worth a visit just to explore or see if there are any souvenirs you want, or a great place to get some fresh fruit or vegetables.

Flinders Street Railway Station- This you will probably see anyway but it really is an amazing building and definitely worth seeing it's located right near St Paul's cathedral,  and is right next to the Yarra River.

*(Flinders street Station, Melbourne)*

Shrine of Remembrance- This is a really cool visit, and definitely worth the walk, it's quite an amazing structure and the walk offers some amazing views of the city too, located just on St Kilda Road. It is now a memorial for all of the men and women who have served in the war, originally built for those who served in World War 1.

*(Shrine of Remembrance, Melbourne)*

Walk along the Yarra River- This really is a beautiful place to walk along I recommend walking down one side past the AAMI park until you get to Morrel bridge, then cross over the bridge and walk back down the other side, through the botanical gardens which are on the way and a good place to stop to eat, then back down the other side until you get to Hamer Hall then you will be back in the city centre near Flinders Street station. This walk offers some great views of the city and the river.

Hosier Lane- This is a must see and really is pretty amazing it is a series of back alleys near Flinders Street Station where the walls are covered top to bottom in graffiti, there are some amazing pieces of art on the walls, and sometimes you can even see people adding to the collection. You could spend a fair bit of time here just looking at the graffiti art work.

*(Hosier Lane Graffiti, Melbourne)*

St Kilda Beach- St Kilda Beach is located 6 Kilometres from Melbourne city centre. It is Melbourne 's most famous beach, there is a pier with a pavilion on the end. When I went here in late February it was quite cold and you could see little penguins in the rocks around the pier which was pretty cool. To get there from the city you can get a bus or train. We hired the local cycles, that are on the street corners, and cycled there it allowed us to see a bit more of Melbourne and the suburbs, and also meant we could cycle along the beach front. St Kilda beach is also really popular for windsurfing which is great to watch, so definitely head to St Kilda for a day.

Get Coffee- Melbourne's coffee is rated some of the best in the world and with no shortage of coffee shops it's definitely a must try, there are loads of little back alley coffee shops around or even ones on the main high street, but it's fair to say Melbourne's coffee is outstandingly good.

Hiking/Walking:

Dandenong Ranges National Park- The Dandenong ranges truly are spectacular and is a must visit while you are in Melbourne, you can get a train from Flinders Street Station to Belgrave Station which will take about an hour and 15 minutes and cost about $12 return. Belgrave is a nice little town again with quaint coffee shops and second hand book stores as well as some larger stores. There are a range of walks that go from Belgrave which you can search online. Belgrave is home to the puffing billy railway being the worlds oldest steam locomotive you can go on it and through the Dandenong ranges either a single journey and walk back or a return trip. It is quite expensive and an adult return will cost you about $50. The Dandenong ranges are famous for the numerous mountain ash trees which can grow up to 20m tall. There are also other places in the Dandenong ranges you can go to, even more so if you have a car, just do a search on Google, and loads of walks and trails will come up and with where to start from.

Yarra Valley- The Yarra Valley which is famous for its wine and wine valleys also offers some incredible walks. This is reachable by public transport but you may have to take a train then a bus. The most popular place to go would be Yarra Glen. It would take you about an hour and 15 minutes by train and bus. The Yarra Valley is relatively flat scenery with few trees unlike the Dandenong rainforest, again walks and trails can be found by just a quick search online. You could also do a wine tour of the Yarra valley which can be purchased online for around $80 which offers a full day of walking around the valley and wine tasting, and looking around the wineries. The Yarra Valley is also quite popular for hot air balloons which you can go in and take a trip over the Yarra Valley which again looks like it offers amazing views, you can take these trips at sunrise, sunset or during the day, they do come with a hefty price tag though, costing around $250 for one trip.

Other things to do in Melbourne:

Eureka Skydeck- This is a 297.3m tall building and offers amazing views of Melbourne city. You can also go in something called the edge which is a glass box which sticks out from the building and it's also the worlds only moving glass structure, you can see straight down beneath yourself. The Skydeck is $20 for an Adult to go up, and to do the edge will cost you an additional $12.

Melbourne Zoo- Another zoo with a range of animals such as Elephants, Hippos, Rhinos, Monkeys. Would be nice to visit for a day out if you lived in Melbourne. Tickets for Adults are $31.60, and offers you unlimited entry throughout the day. You can get to Melbourne zoo very easily by public transport tram or the bus and it takes around 10 minutes.

Lunar Park- Very similar to Sydney's lunar park, but just in Melbourne. Offers a range of rides, it is located in St Kilda at the end of the beach. An unlimited ride ticket for an Adult is $49.50. There is only about 15 rides at the park, but it is nice for a fun evening out.

Melbourne Cricket Ground- If your a fan of cricket or even sports in general this is a good place to visit. A tour of the stadium for an adult is only $22, or you can get a tour of the cricket ground and the national sports museum for $30. It is definitely worth a visit being the largest cricket ground in Australia, infact the largest in the Southern Hemisphere and the $10^{th}$ biggest cricket ground in the world. This is about a 25-30 minute walk from the city centre along the Yarra River, or you could get a tram and it would take about 10 minutes.

Puffing Billy railway- Located in the Dandenong Rainforest at Belgrave Station as mentioned above. It would take about an hour and 30 minutes to get there.

The train route goes through the Dandenong rainforest, under the mountain ash trees, and runs from Belgrave to Gembrook, while passing through Sherwood forest and going over the famous trestle bridge which is just over 90m long also while going over three other timber bridges. The complete journey one way is 24km (15miles). There are a range of different packages on the train but a simple return from Belgrave to Gembrook will cost you $68. If you wanted to experience it but didn't want to pay $68 you could get a single ticket and walk the other way back, giving you the best of both worlds.

Great Ocean Road- A very famous one and you've probably heard of this before you even get to Australia, a lot of people come to Melbourne just to do the great ocean road as it is a good starting point. It is one of the worlds most scenic roads. It is 243km long (151 miles) and stretches along the south eastern coast of Australia, primarily going between Torquay and Allansford. There are a range of prominent landmarks along the way including the twelve apostles, the grotto, London arch, Apollo Bay and Port Campbell. You can do this in a variety of ways, the best choice would be to rent a van and camp in it along the way, or hire/buy a car and drive it, stopping at camp sites, which are plentiful along the great ocean road. You would be able to drive it stopping at all the main places in 3 days, but I would recommend taking at least a week if not longer especially if you are driving from Melbourne, as this then gives you time to see all the sights and explore. Being able to take full advantage of all the great ocean road has to offer. Melbourne is only 100km (62 miles) away, so it's best to start in Melbourne and drive. You can even walk the distance camping along the way, although a much less chosen choice will save you money and give you a completely different experience. The great ocean road offers a range of scenic beaches, rainforests, quaint towns and incredible coastline. Also giving you the opportunity to see some wildlife with dolphin and whale sightings often, and kangaroos and koalas plentiful along the side of the roads and in the rainforests.

Melbourne’s Crown Casino- If you fancy something a bit different and are feeling a little bit lucky, then the crown casino in Melbourne might be a good choice. It's the biggest casino in Australia so is definitely the place to gamble. Located on Southbank and within walking distance from the city also makes it a great choice.

Melbourne Docklands- Although not mentioned very often it is just a short 20 minute tram ride from the city and is in the free tram zone. It lets you see a different side to Melbourne, and is great to have a look around, explore and look at some of the yachts. If your days are already busy it looks beautiful at night, so could be an option for a walk and some late night drinks.

Again these are just a few of the most popular things you can do in Melbourne just skimming the surface. There is so much more to do and it depends on what sort of things you like and enjoy doing yourself. Another thing you might want to look for are rooftop bars. Melbourne is quite famous for its rooftop bars and concerts so it's definitely worth looking them up.

## Chapter 34-Travelling the East Coast

The east coast of Australia, possibly one of the most famous routes for backpackers to travel, with an extensive range of activities, places to stop and people to meet. For the purpose of the majority I am going to go from South to North, so from Sydney to Cairns as this is the most popular route, but if you are going from Cairns to Sydney all the information is still the same you just obviously use it from the bottom to the top starting with Cairns. The east coast of Australia is an incredible trip and there are a lot of different ways in which you can do it.

As mentioned in the transport section of the book, you may want to take the bus and stay in hostels which is what I decided to do as it gives you the opportunity to meet loads more people and is cheaper and less hassle. Another option is to get a van or car, giving you more flexibility with where you go and how long you stay in each place. If you don't have the time to do the full east coast all at once because you are working or just want to visit a few places you could also just take little trips inbetween, going to each place individually for a weekend or a few days inbetween work which many of my friends did.

There are also a lot of options in regards to booking your east coast trip. You can book it all as you go just booking your transport and the hostels a few days in advance, booking activities once you get there. Another option which is what we did and a lot of backpackers choose to do is to book a package. With a package you can tailor make it to suit your needs, so everything from your transport, accommodation, activities and the places you stop. They also give you a plan of where you are going and how many nights you are staying in each place, again which you can tailor to your needs. You can also select a time frame for how long you want to spend travelling the east coast and it is entirely up to you. I would recommend a month as this gives you plenty of time to see everything and also chill out and explore but I would say you would need at least 3 weeks to be able to see and do everything on offer. Another option would be doing half and half so booking some parts of your trip and then leaving others for when you get there. The best part of booking a package is you can get great deals when booking everything with one company, you know it is all booked and everything is paid for before you go. You also know how much it is going to cost and know you only have your food and drink to pay for during the rest of the trip. The average cost of travelling the east coast for a month is around $2500 without food and drink. We paid $1800 for our month trip and a few activities. Below I will go through all the places you can stop and what there is to do in each place.

The list below is the most popular places to stop and things you can do in each of those places, plus what I thought about them. There are more places and a lot of these towns you may not want to stop at, but you can make a decision based on the needs of your trip and any extra research you do.

Sydney- This will obviously be the first place you stop or where you start from. You may have been here for months working or may have come to Sydney purposely to start your east coast adventure. Things you can do in Sydney are mentioned earlier in the book in chapter 32.

Port Macquarie- Is located 390km (242miles) north of Sydney and is probably one of the first places you might like to stop. It is not very touristy and not many backpackers stop here. Port Macquarie is a pretty small town and there are not loads of things to do here apart from beaches and a few walk/hikes in the national park along the coast or to tacking point lighthouse. If you wanted to stop here I would say a couple of days would be enough maybe even just one.

Byron Bay- Byron Bay is about 12 hours north of Sydney by bus and is most travellers first stop when going up the east coast, the majority of people do a night bus from Sydney to Byron Bay. Byron bay was my favourite place along the coast, it had so much to do, good party's and we saw loads of cool stuff while we were there. There are quite a few things you can do while in Byron Bay:

- Surfing- Byron Bay is a popular spot and has a huge beach that stretches along the coast, a lot of the hostels let you borrow surfboards for free, or you can rent them down at the beach or in the town. You might even want to try a surf lesson here.
- Lighthouse Trail- This is a really nice walk along the beach then up to the

lighthouse in Byron, it is particularly nice if you go for sunrise or sunset. It offers amazing views of beaches and the sea and lots of opportunity too see wild animals, and also is Australia's most eastern point along the way. We saw a whale and dolphins when we did this walk.

*(View on the walk to the Lighthouse)*

- Tea Tree Lake- This is quite far from Byron Bay town centre but is definitely worth the trip. You can hire some bicycles and bike there cycling along the beach which is also pretty cool. Our hostel had complimentary bikes but you can hire them for around $10 for a few hours in the town. It takes just 30 minutes to cycle to the lake. It is cool because the lakes water appears to be black but it is infact orange and is to do with the tea trees that surround the lake, it's a great place to chill out and explore.

*(Tea Tree Lake, Byron Bay)*

- Sea Kayaking- This is quite a popular choice with travellers, particularly to see dolphins, a lot of people say they are successful and see them while kayaking. We had a group of dolphins swim past us while we were paddling out on our surfboards, so there is a good chance you might. Sea kayaking costs about $30 for a tour that lasts an hour.
- Nimbin Trip- Take a trip to Nimbin for the day, this is a little hippie town located a couple of hours inland from Byron bay. You can take a trip here for around $25 and it includes a BBQ dinner and a trip to a waterfall as well as a few hours around Nimbin. Nimbin is mostly famous for a little green plant, and the range of products it has in relation to this, which includes cakes and cookies. As well as that it is a really vibrant colourful little town and well worth a visit.

You can also just chill on the beach in Byron, it has an amazing choice of spots on the beach to pick from. The party's in Byron bay are also great and there is a range of places which you can pick from, the best place in my opinion any night of the week would be cheeky monkeys. They have a range of games and stuff going on throughout the night which are loads of fun, and it's a great place to meet loads of other backpackers too, I would say spend at least 3 days here. We spent 3 days and it's one of the only places we could have done with longer maybe even 4 or 5 days so you get to see and fully enjoy Byron bay.

Gold Coast/Surfers Paradise- This is big city, rather different from Byron bay it felt a bit like what Miami would be like, I wasn't a huge fan of Surfers paradise and it felt a bit fake even though it was a beautiful city. There is quite a lot to do here but a lot of it is quite costly other than just spending time on the beach.

- Beaches- Relax on one of the many beaches, there are loads to choose from and the beaches really are amazing, with the city right next to the beaches it's a great place to just relax and chill out. One of the best beaches is Broadbeach and it's located just in front of the city.

*(Broadbeach, Surfers Paradise)*

- Wet n Wild Gold Coast- A water park in the gold coast again another great trip out, but costs a large $75. This entirely depends on your budget, but looks great fun.
- Springbrook National Park- This is probably best accessible if you hire a car for the day, or are doing the east coast trip in a van or car. But offers some amazing walks, waterfalls and swimming holes.

Apart from that there is not a great deal to do in the Gold Coast other than some other theme parks and attractions such as Warner Bros. Movie Park and Dreamworld, which unless you have quite a big budget and a lot of time you'll probably want to skip. There are quite a lot of places to party when in the Gold coast, again it is pretty expensive a bit like Sydney's prices but a lot of fun.

Brisbane- Brisbane is the Capital of Queensland and will be your last big city stop if you're heading up the coast. There are a range of things you can do in

Brisbane, I didn't spend long here at all as found it just like any other city, and wanted to spend more time in other places.

- Australia Zoo- This is probably one of the most famous zoo's in Australia, also know as home of the crocodile hunter (Steve Irwin). This is just north of Brisbane, a couple of hours by bus and is definitely worth a stop for the day trip. There are a range of animals at the zoo and it is particularly famous for its interaction you can have with the animals, such as holding koalas, lizards, spiders, snakes and other native Australian animals. It is pretty expensive at $59 for an Adult but is definitely worth it if you want that all Australian experience, and the chance to get hands on with the animals.
- Brisbane Botanical Gardens- The botanical gardens in Brisbane are pretty small when compared with the likes of Sydney, but they are definitely worth a little visit situated just on the river.
- South Bank Parkland's- A really nice part of Brisbane to just chill out and relax, there is a lagoon for swimming, a fake beach and sand, and some grass areas for relaxing in the sun. It is situated just on the river so it a great place if you just want to chill out in the city.
- Lola Pine Koala Sanctuary- This is the worlds largest koala sanctuary and allows you to have close encounters with Australian wildlife including kangaroos. They also have things like live snake and platypus feeding and it's pretty cheap at only $30 for an Adult.
- Walk along the river- Just have a walk along the river and take in some of the views, also explore and have a walk around the city.

Noosa- Noosa is another one of my favourite places in Australia. It has some amazing beaches, national parks, rivers and is just and all round beautiful place.

- Surfing- Noosa is probably one of the last places you will be able to surf if heading up the east coast of Australia. As there are less waves and there are crocodiles in the water, so definitely take advantage of the surf. I found the surf really good in Noosa probably some of the best while I was in Australia, so if you surf, it's definitely worth a paddle out.

- Noosa National Park- Take a hike around Noosa national park with some amazing views and beaches along the way. There are a range of different walk lengths, all of which can be reached from the main town and vary from 2-3 hours to all day hikes of 5-6 hours, the national park is pretty big and there are lots of cool things to see.

*(Walk along the coast, Noosa National Park)*

- Kayaking- In my opinion this is a must do. You can either go Kayaking in the ocean or in the Noosa rivers. We went kayaking around the rivers and it was amazing, and one of the highlights of my trip. There are so many little rivers and choices of areas to kayak, ranging from little bits of river to huge wide rivers before it goes out to sea, where there is a sand bank. There are also some amazing houses around this area that you will get to see when kayaking. You can rent the kayaks for around $20 for 2 hours which is plenty of time to be out on the water and see everything you would want to see.

*(Kayaking in Noosa)*

- Sunshine Beach- A really nice beach to chill out on if you don't feel like doing any strenuous activities, just go and top up on your tan, read a book or hang out with friends.
- Noosa Everglades- The Noosa Everglades are another trip on offer, there are a range of trips from camping for 2 nights, where you learn survival skills, and go kayaking and canoeing around the Everglades on tours. There are also day trips some which have tour guides others where they are self guided and you are given a map. A one day self guided tour will

cost you around $100, a 2 day guided tour will cost you around $300 and a 2 say self guided tour will cost you around $150, again it depends on your budget and if you really want to see them.

There isn't really much in regards to night life in Noosa, there are a couple of places such as in Nomads hostel there are sometimes some party's but it never gets very busy and there are also a couple of pubs, but nothing compared to Brisbane or Byron bay. I would just take the time to chill out maybe a few beers and a BBQ on the beach before you hit up some of the livelier places up north.

Rainbow Beach or Hervey Bay- Rainbow beach or Hervey bay, these are the one of the two places you will stop before going to Fraser Island. You won't want to stop here unless you are going to Fraser Island as there isn't much to do at all, infact we stopped at Rainbow beach and it was raining, it was a kind of depressing place. You will only want one night before you go to Fraser Island and one night when you get back, maybe a day at the most in Rainbow Beach. At Rainbow beach you can go to the great sand bowl, which is a huge sand bowl, ask your hostel if they have some sand boards and do some sand boarding which is pretty fun, other than that there is a beach which is nothing spectacular. Again at Hervey Bay there is nothing really to do other than the beach. It is just a stop of before going to Fraser island. In regards to partying there is not much going on either, we just played table tennis and pool and got an early night ready for the trip to Fraser Island.

Fraser Island- Fraser island is another must stop, being the largest sand island in the world and stretching over 120km. There are a range of tours that go from either Rainbow Beach or Hervey Bay. The tours usually run for 2 nights/3 days and include all your food, accommodation and transport from your hostel in either Hervey Bay or Rainbow Beach including the ferry. It is a pretty expensive trip being around $300 but does include everything other than alcohol. On the trips if you are over 21 you can drive the 4×4 vehicles down the beach or through the rainforests which is pretty cool, if not it's still amazing and you will have a group of around 6-7 people in each vehicle. You can play music and drink while in the car and you stop at some incredible places around the island such as different lakes, like lake McKenzie and ship wrecks as well as other little gulleys, waterfalls and scenic walks it really is so much fun. There will usually be about 4-5 4×4 vehicles in a group and this whole group will camp and party together at night, you will also cook your food and stuff together. It's great fun and a good way to meet some awesome people and see some incredible sights.

*(Lake McKenzie, Fraser Island)*

Bundaberg- Bundaberg is a place you might want to stop if you want to see what

Australia's rural farm towns are like. If you have done your farm work you wont want to stop here as there is nothing much to do other than just see what Australian farming life is like. You wouldn't want more than a day here just to experience it. Also home to the famous Bundaberg rum, so if you like rum, you might want to take a trip to the distillery.

Airlie Beach- Airlie beach is another really nice town. It is pretty small mainly just made up of one strip but offers some great night life, beautiful weather and this is also where you will head to the Whitsunday Islands from.

- Airlie Beach Lagoon- Airlie Beach has a beautiful lagoon for swimming and some grass areas around the outside, with artificial sand great again for chilling out and topping up on your tan. There is also a beach just around the corner, it is really small and it is recommended that you don't swim in the sea because of crocodiles. But is still a nice place to relax, there are also some BBQ spots around which are nice in the evenings.

*(Airlie Beach Lagoon)*

- Shute Harbour- Take a walk, cycle or get a taxi up to Shute Harbour. To walk it will take you around 2 hours but it's only around 15 minutes in a car. Offers amazing views of the reef, and looks even more incredible for sunset.
- Rent a car and explore some of the rainforests or waterfalls. We hired a Jeep for the day and took it out to some waterfalls and swimming holes, there are also loads of other little beaches around Airlie, which are accessible with a car and make for great sunset spots.

Other than that Airlie Beach is just a great place to party and chill out, before you head to the Whitsundays or when you get back.

Whitsunday Islands- The Whitsunday islands consist of 74 islands and are a massive stretch of coral that is teeming with marine life. This is a must visit when your travelling the east coast. There are a range of trips available such as single day trips from around $100 which go to mainly whitehaven beach and one or two snorkelling stops. And then there are 3 day/2 night trips which is what we chose to do, which cost anywhere from $280 to around $400 depending on the type of boat you go with and what it includes. They include all your food and trips around the Whitsundays, including whitehaven beach, multiple snorkelling trips, walks and sunsets which are truly spectacular. It really is an incredible experience, and also voted one of the best beaches in the world, I would highly recommend spending a couple of nights on a boat when doing this trip rather than just for a day so you get to see a range of sights and it actually gives you enough time to enjoy the sights rather than just rush your way through it. Again in the evening there is the chance for some partying and drinking but this highly depends on the type of boat your on, there are some specific party boats some middle type ones which have drinking but not as excessively, and then also boats which don't really have any and are full of older people, it's entirely dependent on what you yourself want and the kind of experience you want, but it's definitely a must do.

*(Whitehaven Beach, Whitsunday Islands)*

Bowen- Bowen again is a farm town with a very small population, if you have done your farm work and experienced farm life you wont want to stop here at all as there isn't much to do. There are a few walks and hikes through the bush, and also some beaches, but you wouldn’t want to spend long here, and it's not a must stop.

Townsville- Townsville is more of an industrial town, it is not very popular with backpackers, but might be worth a stop for a day or two if you have the time. I didn't stop here on my east coast trip, but I did have a wander round before for about half a day.

- The Strand- Is the forefront of the beach, and has views of the port and Magnetic Island. It is not amazing but is worth a walk down if you have the time.
- Reef HQ- Tickets cost $28 for an Adult, this might be worth a stop if you've got some time in Townsville. It is an Aquarium home to a range of sea life and has a turtle hospital. Also voted the 7th best Aquarium in the South Pacific.

If you have more time in Townsville head to the riverway which is a swimming area located by the river. It has parks and grass areas for relaxing. You could also check out the Queens Gardens which are some botanical gardens located north of Townsville CBD. Many travellers stop in Townsville just for a couple of hours while waiting for the ferry to Magnetic Island, which is perfect as gives you a little while to have a look around.

Magnetic Island- Magnetic Island is an island located 8km offshore from Townsville. Magnetic island offers beautiful unspoiled beaches, hikes, wildlife, and easy access to the great barrier reef. Many people get the ferry from Townsville. A standard return ticket will cost you around $32 to the island and then you will have to pay for your accommodation and any activities you want to do while on the island. There are a range of hostels and hotels on the island ranging in price, the average hostel price is around $30 and for a hotel room will be around $60. There is a massive range of things you can do on Magnetic Island:

- Snorkelling/Diving Trips
- Hiking/Walking through the National Parks
- Visit the Beaches

- Water Sports
- Play some Golf
- Go Horseback Riding
- Kayaking and Canoeing
- Bungalow Bay Koala Village- Where you can hold Koalas, Snakes, Lizards and other animals.
- Go Fishing
- Have a BBQ
- Full Moon Party

With so much to do on Magnetic Island it is definitely worth a stop along your east coast trip, even more so that it is relatively inexpensive to get to the island.

Mission Beach- Mission beach is a small village inbetween Cairns and Townsville, it is not very big and there is not a great deal to do here other than the beach. Most people that do stop here, stop to do a Skydive as it gives you the chance to land on the beach and jump out of a plane over the Great Barrier Reef, which is awesome. It's highly recommended and is rated as one of the best places in Australia to do a skydive. A Tandem skydive over mission beach from 14,000 feet will cost you around $350, and it all depends on your budget as to whether you can afford to do it or not. Other things to do around mission beach, are again chilling out on the beach and hikes and walks around the beautiful rainforests, other than that it's your average Australian beach village.

Cairns- Finally what will be your last stop along the coast, or your first if you're starting from Cairns and working to Sydney. There is loads to do in Cairns, from trips, places to relax and parties, plus the weather is always warm. I would recommend spending at least 5 days in Cairns, that may sound a lot but you will see why you'll need that long after seeing all the stuff there is to do here, if you can spend longer, a week or so would be perfect and give you a good chance to do a bunch of stuff.

- Cairns Lagoon- Maybe for an afternoon or even a day, chill out at Cairns Lagoon, it's located right near the sea, near the centre of Cairns. It is a great place to go swimming, chill out and there are even multiple free BBQs located down the front which are brilliant if you want a BBQ and some beers one night. There is also often a Market around the lagoon which could be worth checking out.

*(Cairns Lagoon)*

- Play Volleyball- There are three volleyball courts down the promenade just past the skate park about a 10 minute walk from Cairns centre. So if your feeling active some volleyball on the beach front in the sun might do the job.
- Cairns Night Markets- Cairns night market is open every day of the year

from around 9pm, and offers a range of products, foods and even things like massages so is worth a look around to see if there is anything you fancy.

- Diving/Snorkelling the Great Barrier Reef- This is a must do while you're in Australia, The Great Barrier reef, the largest living organism in the world and even being visible from space. It is a 2,300km-long ecosystem and comprises of thousands of reefs and hundreds of islands that are made of over 600 types of coral. It's home to countless species of colourful fish, molluscs, starfish, turtles, dolphins and sharks. There are a range of different trips that go from Cairns such as day snorkelling trips, day diving trips and even trips for 2-3 days. Unless you are an avid diver I would just recommend going out on a day trip as there is so much to do in Cairns and this will still give you the chance to see everything you need to see. Day snorkelling trips cost around $100 and include all your equipment, lunch, snacks and around 3 snorkelling stops. Dive day trips cost around $200 and will include 2 dives, and a snorkelling stop, as well as all equipment, lunch and snacks. Prices do vary greatly, but it depends on the type of boat your going on some are very fancy and which dive sites you go to etc. If you have never dived before you can do a trial dive, which will cost a little less but you will only usually get one dive not 2, unless you pay extra, again there is a lot of leverage dependent on your preference.

*(Diving, Great Barrier Reef)*

- Daintree Rainforest- This is the largest tropical rainforest in Australia. Again is definitely worth a visit and there are a range of trips going to the rainforest which include hiking through the rainforest, waterfalls, swimming holes and most of them include a BBQ lunch. Tours cost around $100 for the day but again vary depending on the tour and what it includes, they all also include transport to and from the rainforest. Alternatively if you are over 21 and there is a group of you, you could hire a car can drive out there yourself this way it would save you a lot, but you would have to find out some hikes and walks yourself which go to waterfalls etc. Which can be easily found on Google. Hiring of a car would be around $60 for the day so between four people with fuel would be pretty cheap, you could also take a BBQ and some beers and do it yourself.

- Kuranda Scenic Railway- Take a trip on the Kuranda Railway. It takes you from Cairns to Kuranda, which is a village in the rainforest, and offers a truly spectacular trip through a world heritage-listed rainforest, it passes through waterfalls and the Barron gorge. It is a 25km (15 mile) trip and takes around 90 minutes by the train, you can also drive in around 15 minutes. A day trip from Cairns will cost around $115, which includes pick up from your hostel, a ride on the Kuranda railway and gives you time to explore the markets and town of Kuranda.
- Cape Tribulation- Cape Tribulation is 110km (68 miles) North of Cairns. It is located within the Daintree Rainforest and is where the rainforest meets the ocean, this again is another world heritage area. There are a range of tours going here as with any of the activities, such as staying overnight in cabins in the rainforest which sounds pretty fun, and there are also day trips. Again prices vary but the average day trip price will be around $100, that includes transport, a drive up the coast and a guided rainforest walk. For a 2 day one night trip it will cost you around $150 and is basically the same trip with a little longer in each place you stop, and a night in a Cabin in the Rainforest. Alternatively you could hire a car and head there yourselves, this way it gives you a bit more freedom.
- Atherton Tablelands- The Atherton Tablelands are a highland region just

west of Cairns. Again has a range of beautiful walks, through the rainforest, with waterfalls and a range of animals, birds and swimming spots. There are a range of tours that again go here costing around $100, including a walk through the rainforest, a number of stops at waterfalls, lakes, swimming spots and lookout views. Or you could hire a car between a group of you and head there yourself, there are loads of circuits passing through waterfalls that are signposted which you could easily do yourself without the need for a guide.

- Fitzroy Island- Fitzroy Island is only 45 minutes from Cairns and is an idyllic tropical paradise, trips here range in price depending on the activities you choose to do. Ranging from around $70 for just a trip to the island and you do what you want when you get there to around $100 which includes 2 activities which can be a range of things, from a glass bottom boat tour, to kayak hire for two hours, or paddle board hire for two hours amongst other things. You can just pay for your tickets and see what you feel like doing when you get there. There are plenty of places to hire from, apart from this there are walks and beaches to relax on. I would say a day is all you need to explore the island, a day trip will give you about 7 hours on the island.
- Cairns Botanical Gardens- Cairns Botanical Gardens in my eyes is a must visit, firstly because it is free and gives you an insight into the tropical rainforest. There are a range of walks which are easily navigable among the rainforest on board walks. Among the rainforest are streams and lakes, at one particular lake, you will easily recognize it there is a small bridge going over it if you take some bread and drop it into the water turtles will come to feed which is pretty cool, also watch out for other birds and animals such as Pelicans. It's open from 7.30am to 5.30pm every day and is about a 30 minute walk from the centre of Cairns. You could even hike up the hill which gives you some amazing views of the

sea and airport. You can walk to botanical gardens down the Esplanade, which also gives you the opportunity to walk all the way down the esplanade taking in the views.

*(Cairns Botanical Gardens)*

- Fishing- There are also a range of fishing trips available, again ranging in price depending on what you are fishing for, they are usually quite expensive and range from $150 to some trips around $400, there are also half day trips available as well as full day.
- Water Sports- There are also a range of water sport activities you can do such as jet skiing, there are also jet skiing tours available which take you looking for crocodiles, if you are interested in water sports, just ask at any of the travel shops and they will give you more information, on what's available and how much they cost.

The night life in Cairns is also very good with a wide choice of places to go including a large casino which shows sports and is a good way to get out if it's raining. The main places you will go out would be Gilligan's and the Woolshed, places to go out was in Chapter 5 if you want somewhere to go out. With the trips they do range in price, the prices i stated is just the average prices, again it depends what time of the year it is, and if you book a lot of trips together you should be able to get a deal, so don't be scared to haggle. There are loads of travel shops specifically for backpackers, located around the cities/towns which will be selling trips so make sure you look around and check prices to see what they offer and what deals you can get, you will know which stores I am talking about as soon as you get to Australia.

## Chapter 35-Travelling the West Coast

The west coast of Australia is usually a lot less explored than the east coast, and has a lot less of a backpacker scene. This means a lot less choice in hostels, transport and partying. Saying that doesn't mean it's not worth doing, it is still a beautiful part of Australia, a lot more quite and peaceful and will maybe offer you a different insight into Australian culture and the beauty of down under. Again there are a few options in regards to travelling the west coast. One option and the most popular would be to rent a car/van, or buy one if you have the chance and travel up the coast in that, this gives you a lot more opportunity to get around, and see the sights that are often off the beaten track, and the places where buses wont take you. The second option would be to use the bus, even though the west coast is a lot less popular with backpackers, it still has an extensive bus network throughout the coast and inland, and offering reasonable prices, which are talked about in the transport section of the book. You can book a package as with the east coast so a bus heading from Perth to Broome and you can then stop off where you like as long as you keep moving in the right direction, or you could just book your buses separately moving as you go.

Travelling the west coast you will probably want to travel north, as Perth the main city in Australia that you will most likely fly to is situated more to the south and there is a lot more to see north, you could travel south and then back up past Perth to the north but that would mean coming back on yourself, but again it entirely depends on what you want to see. To travel the west coast about three weeks would be a good time and allow you to see most of the main sights, of course you can always spend longer doing it, and spend more time in certain places, this is entirely personal preference and depends on your budget and time scale.

Perth- Perth is a pretty quite city in comparison to the likes of Sydney and Melbourne, but that doesn't mean there's less to do. There are quite a few cool spots to check out if you're in Perth, such as beaches the city itself and there are some pretty awesome viewpoints.

*(Kings Park at Sunset, Perth)*

- Kings Park- This is must stop if you're in Perth, it offers some amazing walks showing off a range of plant, flower and tree species. There are also some outstanding views of Perth city and Swan river. This is a great spot to head to at sunset. There is also a war memorial here and a café, and also something called a whispering wall, which if you talk into at one end of, somebody can hear you at the other end it's pretty cool.
- Perth City- Head into the city itself, do a little exploring, hit the shops or go to some of the nice restaurants in the evening, it's a cool place to have a stroll around during the afternoon.
- The Beaches- Get a train from the central station in Perth to North Fremantle, starting from north Fremantle walk along the beach heading north offers some great views along the beach. Then there is a beach-less section until you get to Cottesloe beach, which was my favourite beach in Perth. It is usually pretty busy but again offers some amazing views, there are also some nice little cafés and Restaurants here if you want something to eat, and some grass areas to chill out if you don't fancy sitting on the beach. This is a great beach to stop and have a swim at. Once you've finished at Cottesloe, it's well worth having a walk through the suburbs, to get a look at some of the houses and the area, it really is a beautiful spot, you can then either hop on the train at Swanbourne Station or Claremont Station which is a little bit further depending on how tired you are, back to the city.
- Surfing- Perth offers some great surf throughout the year, head to Cottesloe beach or Fremantle, surf board hire is available around the beaches at reasonable prices. Cottesloe will be a busier than Fremantle beach so if you're looking for some quieter surf you should head there, this may mean carrying your board further though. If you're new to

surfing there are also surf lessons on offer which may be of interest to you.

- Swan Valley- Swan Valley is at the upper end of the Swan river and is a beautiful part of the west coast and surrounding areas of Perth, there are numerous wineries of which you could pay a visit or even book a trip to in advance, this is a great choice for a day if you feel like getting out of the city. There are a few places you could head to such as Ellenbrook, Jane Brook, Herne Hill, Avery and loads of other suburbs in the area of Swan valley totalling 14. If you decide you want to go to Swan valley you should look at the surrounding suburbs and see which one suits you best for what you want to do. In a car it takes about 30 minutes to drive out to swan valley and on public transport about 45, depending on which suburb you head for. This is a really nice place to go to for walking around and enjoying the countryside around Perth.
- Rottnest Island- This is an island just of the west coast of Australia, about 18km (11miles) from Fremantle. There are daily ferry services to and from Perth so you could go just for the day and explore the island, or stay for a night or two in one of the hotels, even though I think a day would be enough. If you want a guided tour they are available but will cost you more than just the ferry. There is loads to do on the island from walks, cycling, snorkelling among other activities. The island is also home to loads of different animal and plant species and really offers some surreal beauty. There are a number of walks that go around different parts of the island and are of different lengths. The ferry will take you about 25 minutes from Fremantle, 45 from Hillarys boat harbour and 90 from Perth Barrat street jetty. Tours from Perth or Fremantle will cost about $100 and include a free wildlife cruise around the island, they last about 8 hours so this is a pretty good price for everything you are getting. From Fremantle the return to Rottnest island is around $50, so in my opinion

you might as well do the tour as gives you all your transport a cruise and time to explore the island with expert advice.

Going out in Perth can also be a good time, there are going to be a lot less backpackers than along the east coast as mentioned before and price of alcohol in Perth is a little more expensive, but there are still plenty of great places to head out too for a good night. One of the best areas to head to would be Northbridge, there are a range of bars and clubs around here playing different types of music and they're all relativity close so if you don't like one, you can easily head to another. Just to list a few spots you might want to go to in Perth.

- Metro City Club
- Mint Nightclub
- The Shed
- Paramount Nightclub
- Geisha Bar
- Air Nightclub

These are just some popular bars/nightclubs in the northbridge area, but there are loads of other places you could head to such as Fremantle, if your feeling a more relaxed night out or some casual drinks.

Heading South:

Bunbury- This is know as the second capital city of WA. It is a few hours south of Perth and can be reached on the bus, taking around 2-3 hours. There are a few things to do here:

- Kamboona Bay
- Visit the Farmers Market
- Back Beach

- Bunbury Wildlife Park
- Bunbury Lighthouse Lookout

They are the main things you can do in Bunbury, I would recommend maybe just 1 or 2 nights here, You can always relax and there is the opportunity for whale and dolphin watching in this area.

Busselton- Busselton is about an hour south of Bunbury. It is a very small town and there is not a great deal to do here other than the beach. One of the most famous attractions is Busselton jetty. This is a 1.6km long jetty which you can walk along or get the train. Again I would recommend a night here maybe longer if you want to enjoy the beach, which is amazing in the summer.

Margaret River- Margaret River is a town in the south west of Australia, about 5 hours drive by car. It is a beautiful region of the west coast and worth the drive even just to spend a couple of nights here. There are some incredible, secluded beaches here which have some of the best surf in Australia, so if you're a keen surfer it's definitely worth the trip down. Margaret River is also famously known for it's wineries. There are plenty of tours which take you round and let you do wine tasting and show you how they make it etc. Day tours around the wineries start from around $85 and include a lot of wine. Margaret River is also home to a range of caves, the two most well known ones being Mammoth cave and Ngilgi Cave. These caves are worth a visit and are spectacular, but for an adult cost $22.50. It does sound pretty expensive just to go in some caves, but it's 100% worth it, and they're truly are amazing.

Albany- This is about 5 hours down the coast from Margaret River and would probably be your next main stop unless you want to stop for the beaches or views which are beautiful along the way. Again there is not a huge amount to do here for tourists other than just enjoy the natural beauty and relax at the beaches. There a range of beaches to choose from at Albany and they can be found with a quick google search. Here are a few to get you started ranging from beaches, national parks and harbours.

- Greens Pool
- West Cape Howe National Park
- Oyster Harbour
- Two Peoples Bay Nature Reserve
- Torndirrup National Park

Bremer Bay- A very small town in WA, I would recommend one night but is a great stopping point inbetween Albany and Esperance. Again just enjoy the pristine white beaches and the sea. There are also opportunities to do a dive or snorkelling trip. You could also head to the Fitzgerald river national park if you wanted to go walking or hiking.

Esperance- If you are heading south instead of north one place you must stop is in Esperance, which is home to a pink lake, and yes this is a huge lake which water looks pink. It is a big salt lake and is 3km west of Esperance.

Heading North:

Geraldton- This is a quite place north of Perth and maybe one of the first places you would want to stop when heading north. There is not a great deal to do here, some beaches and also a little bit of a harbour but would be worth a walk around.

Kalbarri National Park- Kalbarri National Park is really easy to access as is located just along the coast north of Geraldton. There are loads of walks and hikes throughout the national park, and it is mostly made up of red rock with some rivers and streams running through it. There are also coastal cliffs stretching 100m above the ocean giving some amazing views. There are also lots of gorges and lakes, but it is definitely worth a stop for a day or two to explore some of the trails.

Coral Bay- This may be another place worth stopping on your trip up north, it is not a very populated area, but offers some amazing snorkelling and the opportunity to see hundreds of fish species. Again home to some amazing beaches, but you will see amazing beaches all the way up the west coast, so it's up to you which ones you want to stop at.

Ningaloo Reef- This is a world heritage site and reef, and is famous for sightings of whale sharks and manta rays. The Ningaloo reef is 260km (160 miles) long. As said previously the world heritage sight is most famously known for sightings of whale sharks, the largest known extant fish species. They feed between March and June so this would be the best time to try and see them. During the winter months, the reef is part of the migratory routes for dolphins, dugongs, manta rays and humpback whales. The beaches of the reef are an important breeding ground of the loggerhead, green and hawks-bill turtles. And also home to more than 500 other species of fish. There is plenty of opportunity for snorkelling and diving trips. To make the most out of the reef a diving day trip is definitely recommended. Dive trips to the Ningaloo reef start from around $75 but depend on how many dives you get etc. There are also loads of other specific trips, such as to see specifically whale sharks or manta rays. There are even kayaking/snorkelling trips. You can book these online or there are local dive and tourist shops you could go in and get more information from.

Karijni National Park- The Karijini national park is a must stop while your in western Australia, it is located east inland of Coral Bay about a 10 hour drive, it doesn't look very far on a map but it is a long trip, but a must visit. The national park is made up of gorges, waterfalls and rock pools. It really is in the outback if you want to get that Australian outback experience without going to the centre. There a loads of trails to walk which take you throughout the gorges and to water holes which you can swim. Some of the best waterfalls and swimming holes are the Joffre Falls, Fortescue Falls, Circular Pools and Falls and Fern Pool. Definitely make this a stop as it really is beautiful. I would recommend spending 2-3 or even more nights here doing the various walks and going to different parts of the national park.

*(Karijini National Park Swimming hole and Waterfall)*

Eighty Mile Beach- As described in the name it's a beach which is eighty miles long located between Port Headland and Broome. Worth a stopover on your trip up to Broome as it is a long drive, maybe camp on the beach with a BBQ and just spend the day relaxing.

Broome- This will probably be your last stop in WA, as there is nothing much more north, it is a small town, but a very popular tourist destination. There are a range of things to do in Broome.

- Visit Cable Beach
- Visit the Horizontal Falls
- Cape Leveque

- Dampier Peninsular
- Rosebuck Bay
- Go to a Pearl Farm

That is just to name a few, they are mostly quite relaxed things to do, but offer amazing chances to see some wildlife such as dolphins, crocodiles, camels and different bird species. There is also a lot of opportunity for fishing in Broome, as there is for diving and snorkelling on the mostly untouched coral reefs. There is also the potential to surf in Broome depending on the time of year for the waves, and also the jellyfish migrating, which a lot of locals call stinger season.

These are just the main places to see along the west coast, there are many more less well known places, that may be of interest or of which you may want to visit, listed are the most popular places and things to do.

## Chapter 36-Uluru/The Red Centre

Uluru also known as Ayers rock is another huge tourist attraction in Australia and very popular, the only problem with visiting, is that it literally is in the middle of nowhere, right in the middle of the Australian Outback. The only way to get there is by Train or Flying. You could also drive but this would be a very long arduous trip, throughout the desert and if you broke down, you would be in a spot of bother. Alice Springs is the town where you will most likely stay during your trip to the red centre, you then get a shuttle to Ayers rock when you decide you want to go. A lot of people don't realize how far Ayers rock is from Alice Springs it's actually a 5 hour drive, but you can book trips from Alice springs that include your transport and 2-3 nights at Ayers rock.

*(Ayers Rock, Central Australia)*

Getting to Alice Springs:

Flying- Flights are relatively inexpensive, you should look at flying into Alice Springs, flights from Sydney will take about 2-3 hours and cost you anywhere from $300-$500 for a return trip depending on what kind of times you fly and what deals you can find. This is probably the easiest way to get there.

Driving- Driving is a long choice, to drive to Alice Springs from Melbourne or Sydney it would take you 2-3 days, and the price of fuel is a lot more expensive in the Outback. In fuel it would probably end up costing you about $450 one way, obviously if you split it between a few of you it is going to be a lot cheaper, but it is still expensive especially for the amount of time it is going to take you to get there. It does though give you the opportunity to see the real outback of Australia and make a proper road trip out of it.

Train- Trains are a very expensive way of travelling to Ayers rock. The main train that goes to Ayers rock goes from Adelaide to Darwin and is called the Ghan. Prices are incredibly expensive, more information on the Ghan train can be found in chapter 27 of the book.

Bus- There are no buses directly to Alice Springs from anywhere, the only bus you can take is a greyhound from Alice Springs to Ayers rock, and fares cost around $155.

There are a range of different companies that offer different tours and trips to Ayers rock from Alice Springs, ranging in prices and what you do. A hostel in Alice Springs will cost you around $25 -$30 a night and similar prices for hostels at Uluru, you won't want to spend too long here as there isn't too much to do or see, I would recommend spending a night before you head to Ayers rock and a night or two after.

Tours to Ayers rock range from half day tours to 4 or 5 day tours. I would recommend something like a 3 day tour as will give you long enough to see Ayers rock and a range of other sights.

3 Day Budget Uluru Tour- This will cost you around $350 and is a 3 day tour of the area including 2 nights, all your meals and transport to and from Alice Springs which is a pretty good deal. You get to see some amazing sights such as Uluru, Kings Canyon and Kata Tjuta. You also get informative talks, information and walks around all of the spots. The cool thing about these trips are that you get to camp under the stars, which would be spectacular as there is nearly zero light pollution in the outback. These operate in groups of 15-30 so is also a good chance to meet some new people. Here is a link to some of the Uluru trips and more information- www.uluru.travel

1 Day Budget Uluru Tour- This will cost you around $210 and includes your transport from Alice Springs you also get to see Uluru and Kata Tjuta. Dinner is included.

In my opinion you may as well spend the extra $150 and do the three day trip as it is much better value for money allowing you to spend more time around the sights, includes all your meals and gives you the chance to camp with Ayers rock in the background. You will also get the chance to see Ayers rock change colours, which as the sky changes colour, it looks as if the rock is changing colour. You can climb up Ayers rock but it is recommend that you do not. The local Aboriginals ask that you do not as it is a sacred site to them and also people have died climbing it. So the local government ask that you do not climb it, although it is not illegal. If you do wish to climb it, it will take around 2 hours if you are fit and active. So a complete trip to Ayers rock including flights, a 3 day tour, nights in Alice springs and food would probably cost you about $900 for 5 nights.

## Chapter 37-Other Places Worth Stopping

So listed above are all the main places and cities you might want to stop during your Australia adventure, but there are other amazing places of the beaten track and cities which are less popular and less prone to tourists, which you might want to visit.

Tasmania- Tasmania is an island of the south coast of Australia, and is known for its rugged wilderness. It has a population of just over half a million people over which half live in the state capital, Hobart.

There are only two ways which you can get to Tasmania and that is to fly or to get the ferry, to fly from Sydney it will cost you around $200 to get to Tasmania, and from Melbourne around $120. You can also get a ferry from Melbourne which costs around $56 each way, or if you have a car you can take that across and that costs around $87 each way. You can find more information on the ferry's on this website www.spiritoftasmania.com.au. Hostels again will cost you around the $25 area.

*(Ferry to Tasmania, Melbourne)*

There a range of things to do in Tasmania and places to see which are listed below:

- Fraycinet National Park- Located on the east coast of Tasmania, offers amazing walks, views and chances to see wildlife.

- Port Arthur Historic Site- This is a small town and former convict settlement, this is one of Australia's most significant heritage areas and also offers a museum.
- Salamanca Market- This is a local market held in Hobart on Saturdays between 8am and 3pm.
- Bay of Fires- This is on the north eastern side of Tasmania, and is a region of white beaches and blue waters.
- Royal Tasmanian Botanical Gardens
- Cataract Gorge- This is a gorge 1.5km from Launceston, and is one of the regions premier tourist attractions.
- Russell Falls- These are a cascade of beautiful waterfalls located in the mount view national park.
- Franklin Gordon Wild Rivers National Park- This is a national park located 117km west of Hobart and is named on the two main rivers lying on the bounds of the park. Great for walking and hiking.
- Montezuma Falls- Large waterfall located on the west coast range of Tasmania.
- Tamar Valley- Another amazing spot for taking walks and relaxing, it runs north of the city Launceston, either side of the Tamar river.
- Tasmania Zoo

They are just a few things to do in Tasmania, some of the main things you might want to see such as waterfalls, national parks, markets, towns and gardens. As well as all this stuff to do you should explore the towns and villages, you might also like to take part in some sporting activities like mountain biking and water sports. There are a range of other tourist attractions which you might like to see such as museums and trips but these can be found when you get there.

Canberra- Canberra is Australia's capital, yet it is largely unvisited by backpackers to Australia, probably because there isn't really a backpacker scene and there isn't so much to do. But if you are passing through it, it's worth a stop as there are some cool things to see, and a lot of history to the city.

Things to do in Canberra:

- Australia War Monument-The Australian War Memorial is Australia's national memorial to the members of its armed forces and supporting organisations who have died or participated in wars involving the Commonwealth of Australia.
- National Gallery of Australia- Is the Countries largest art gallery, it is free to enter and is open from 10.am to 5pm.
- National Museum of Australia- This is again free and is open from 9am till 5pm, they say you should book tickets online though as it does get pretty busy, and saves disappointment if it's fully booked.
- Parliament house-The meeting place of the parliament of Australia, definitely worth a look as the building is pretty amazing.
- Australian National Botanical Gardens- This is a really nice place to go for a walk or a chilled out day. There are a range of different walks and even some small water holes and waterfalls.
- Commonwealth Park Canberra- Another nice spot for walking and chilling out it is located on the north side of lake Griffin. There are many small ponds and water features, and also cycle paths and trails.
- Big Splash Water park Canberra- A water park located in Canberra, it has a number of pools and 9 slides. Tickets costs $25 and it is open from 11am till 5pm. The pools just for swimming are open much longer and you can find these on the website. www.bigsplashwaterpark.com.au.It is located just outside the city in the suburb of Macquire.
- Mount Kosciuszko- This is the highest mountain in Australia and is located on the main range of snowy mountains in the Kosciuszko

national park in New South Wales. It stands at a height if 2,228m above sea level. For the more adventurous travellers, you can reach the summit of Mount Kosciuszko, you can drive to a place called Charlotte Pass, from which an 8 kilometre (5mi) path leads to the summit. Anybody with a moderate fitness can reach the summit. It is about a 3-4 hour round trip to the top and back, depending on your fitness and how long you spend at the top. And to drive it's about 2 and a half hours from Canberra to the Charlotte Pass from where you can reach the summit.

Darwin- Darwin is the capital of the northern territory, and is situated on the Timor sea. Darwin is located very close to Asia and has a wet and dry climate so dependent on this, may help you decide when you want to visit. The wet season in Darwin runs from November till April, where it is prone to cyclones, so it would be best to avoid these months of the year. Darwin does stay very hot all year round though.

Things to do in Darwin:
Darwin is relatively small with a population of around 138,000 people so there isn't a great deal for travellers to do. I would say 5 nights would be plenty in this city.

- Mindil Beach- This is a beach located near Darwin's central business district, there is also a sunset market held here which runs from the last Thursday in April till the Last Thursday in November, obviously just not running in the wet season which is another reason to miss Darwin during these months.
- Darwin Military Museum- This is a great visit if you are into history and want to learn more about Darwin's involvement in the various wars. It costs $18 for adults to enter.
- Darwin Territory Wildlife Park- This is a zoo and is located at Berry

Springs, about 60 kilometres (37miles) south of Darwin. It takes about 45 minutes to get there. There are a range of native animals and shows to see. For an adult it costs $26 to go into the wildlife park. The park is open from 8.30 till 6pm and it can be reached by public transport. For more information visit the website. www.territorywildlifepark.com.au/

- Charles Darwin National Park- This is located 4km SE of Darwin. The park has 5 trails which are suitable for bush walking and mountain biking, the national park also offers some amazing views of the city.
- Lake Alexander- This is a man made recreational lake created for the people of Darwin and tourists to enjoy, the water in the lake is refreshed with pumps, and it keeps marine life out such as crocodiles, bull sharks and jellyfish. The lake is also nice to just walk around with there being various gardens where you can relax.
- Just explore the city have a walk around and see some of the buildings.
- Kakadu National Park- Kakadu National Park is a massive nature preserve in the northern territory, with terrain encompassing, wetlands, rivers and sandstone, it's also home to a range of animal species including crocodiles, turtles and hundreds of bird species. It is located 150km to the east of Darwin, and takes about 1 hour 45 minutes to drive there. This is a great day out for bush walking and exploring the wilderness, there are also a range of water holes and waterfalls, although I wouldn't recommend swimming in them like you can in NSW as refreshing as they look, they may be home to salt water crocodiles. In regards to getting there, I would recommend hiring a car and taking a little road trip and splitting the cost between a group of you. You will need someone over 21 to do this though, as is required for car hire. There are also various day tours to the Kakadu, but they are very expensive costing around $170 for a day. It does include a river cruise, food and seeing all the major sights, but for most backpackers that's going to be a bit out of budget, you might

be able to find some cheaper deals, but I would still recommend hiring a car and heading there yourself. The Park is massive stretching 200km North to South and 100km East to West, so research where you want to go before you leave and some things you want to see.

There is also quite a good night life in Darwin with a strip much as to the kind you would find in Spain which runs through the centre of the city, and hosts a number of clubs, bars and restaurants. A couple you might want to check out are Throb, Discovery, Time Nightclub and Shenannigans which is a popular Irish bar. Hostels in Darwin are again, priced similarly the same as other hostels throughout the country costing you around $20 a night.

Adelaide- Adelaide is south Australia's capital, and it is a 7 hour drive from Melbourne, again this is not an extremely popular destination with tourists, as is rather out of the way from everything, being inbetween Perth and Melbourne on the South Coast, it's often a good starting point if you are doing the great ocean road to drive from Adelaide to Melbourne or the other way around.

Things to do in Adelaide:

- Adelaide Zoo- This is the second largest zoo in Australia, and works on a non for profit basis so really is worth a visit if you are here. There are a range of animals including Alligators, Lions, Tigers, Lemurs and over 250 other species. It is open from 9.30 till 5pm and costs $33 for an Adult, and is only a 10 minute walk from the centre.
- Victoria Square- This is the central square of Adelaide, and represents the city's square mile.
- Adelaide Botanical Gardens- This is a 128 acre public garden located in the northern part of the city. This is a really nice place like the other botanical gardens to chill out have a walk around or stop for lunch.

- Adelaide Park Lands- These are parks that surround the centre of the capital, it is kind of a green belt that surrounds the city centre, again great for walks and if you fancy a break from the city.
- Hallet Cove Conservation Park- This is a protected area on the coast 14km (22 miles) south of the city centre. It has some amazing walks and views of the ocean so is a good half day or even day out if you want to get out of the city.
- Walk through Port Adelaide- Discover Adelaide's 19th century buildings, pubs and wharves in this old part of the city.
- Adelaide's Central Market- Visit the Market which sells a range of fresh fruits and vegetables, seafood, cheeses and artisan food.
- Visit the beaches- Head to one of Adelaide's many popular beaches. Enjoy the hustle and bustle of Glenelg, or the laid-back vibe of Henley and Grange with wooden piers, beach side cafés and old-school pubs.
- Shark Cage Diving- This is if you fancy a bit of an adrenaline rush, head to Port Lincoln. The only place you can cage dive with sharks in Australia. There are a range of ways to get to Port Lincoln from Adelaide, you can fly which takes about 45 minutes. The best way would be to get a shuttle bus or drive and spend the night in Port Lincoln it takes about 5 hours to drive probably a little longer by bus. Flights will cost you about $100 for a return to and from Adelaide, and the bus would be about $50 return. You can do a shark cruise, and cage dive for a full day it would cost you about $250, this includes all the equipment you may need and lunch.

## Before You Go

So that's it, pretty much everything you need to know about Australia, from places to go, how to get a job and how much things cost, with all this stuff you are pretty much set up for the best time of your life in Australia. This next chapter covers things unrelated to Australia, but essential things that will be very useful in making your time in Australia much more enjoyable, and giving you the best out of the experience.

## Chapter 38-My Mistakes

Now, I definitely made some mistakes when I was travelling, being away from home for a year with only myself to rely on it was kind of expected I would have some hiccups along the way. Fortunately it was nothing major, and I can guarantee that you will make your own mistakes. Below are a few examples of mistakes I made and how to avoid them, so hopefully you wont make the same ones… you'll just have your own.

One of the first mistakes I made was regarding my luggage, I booked a flight to Australia and for some crazy reason I was allowed 40kg of luggage from 2 pieces of baggage including hand luggage. So I decided to use it all and took 2 massive suitcases with me, which turned about to be an absolute nightmare, getting around easily with them, manoeuvring through hostels, walking around the streets, it was just a complete nightmare. I ended up sacking one of the suitcases of after my first week and condensing my stuff down, getting rid of all the stuff I didn't need. Only take the essential stuff, if worst comes to worst and you find out you need something which you didn't think you would, you can always buy it when you get to Australia. After about 6 weeks I decided to ditch the other suitcase which was partially broken anyway, and get a backpack, this literally made my life so much easier. It was an 80 litre backpack, and I got it of ebay for around $50, I still have it today. Using an actual backpack makes it so much easier to travel around, get places and move about so whatever you do, use a backpack and not a suitcase, it will make your life so much easier.

Another thing I did on various occasions was book transport particularly flights or buses and then not actually end up getting them, which probably ended up costing me about $500 in total. The thing when travelling is your plans are constantly changing, you meet people who give you new ideas, or you get offered a better higher paid job than the one you just got offered, and you will often end up changing your plans last minute. What I would recommend is if you are not 100% sure you are going to be doing something, like incredibly certain, wait a little while and see if your plans do change if they don't then all good book away. Another thing you can do especially if you are booking a flight is pay for a cancellation refund, this is usually about $20 depending on the cost of the flight, but then if you cancel your flight you will get a 100% refund and this could end up saving you a lot of money, again it's your individual choice but trust me when I say your plans will change.

Wasting your time with commission only jobs. Don't get me wrong sometimes they may work out and actually be good but that is probably 1/100. When I first got to Sydney I just applied to loads of jobs as I wanted anything, I wasn't really bothered at all what I did, and I got loads of interviews for commission only jobs which I travelled to and attended and they always turned out to be a waste of time. I wouldn't go to these or at least quiz them, and ask loads of questions while you are on the phone before you go to an interview so you know if it is worthwhile, this will save you time and money in travelling all the way to the interview. Part salary and part commission jobs are worth going to as give you a basic pay and also the chance to earn extra money as an incentive, so I would definitely check those out.

This you probably already know but it is an important thing to factor in so your not let down. Jobs being described to be a lot better than they actually are, even more so in regards to farm work. It's never going to be as good as how it is described on the advert. Me and a friend applied and took a farm job after only being in Australia a couple weeks. The advert said they have tennis courts, nice accommodation, fully equipped kitchens, swimming pool etc. When infact most of it was all highly exaggerated, the tennis courts that we could use were in the local town which was a couple hours drive away, and we didn't have a car. The accommodation was really poor, the kitchen was in a metal sort of container, and the swimming pool was like a pond interior. They really over sold it and I experienced this with a couple of farms so I would just recommend taking that into consideration.

*(Accommodation on a farm in Queensland)*

We all know that backpackers love to drink, but it can be a particularly risky thing, even more so the night before an early flight. I happened to be very lucky, but I would highly recommend saying no to alcohol if you have to be up early for a flight because it could end up costing you incredibly. Even though this didn't happen to me in Australia, I still think it's important to mention, because as we all know one drink turns into a few drinks and before you know it your out partying which is what happened to me in Bangkok. I woke up an hour before my flight was leaving to Indonesia, luckily I made it just in time but quite often people don't and this can end up being even more serious if you are on a visa and have a limited stay, because if you miss your flight you could end up being in that country illegally. Not only that but it's going to cost you more money, which you might not have to spend. In the worst case scenario you might end up not even being able to go on that trip you saved and planned for.

When it comes to washing and drying your clothes when your travelling, a lot of people leave them out to dry on washing lines in hostels outside and then go and collect them once they have dried. I once did this at a hostel in Airlie beach only to come back and find all of my clothes had gone, which was incredibly annoying as it meant that I had to go and buy all new clothes. This was the only time I had a problem with it, you will usually be fine and nobody will take anything, but it can happen and is something to be aware of. I would recommend if you don't want to pay for a dryer, like we didn't because we were trying to save money, either just paying and using a dryer or hanging your stuff in your room over the balcony. This way if anything does go missing you know that it's someone in the room. This only happened to me once and I think 99% of the time nobody is going to steal your stuff as travellers are pretty honest, but its something to think about and worth a mention.

## Chapter 39-Before You Go Check list

There are a number of things you will want to have sorted and done before you leave for Australia, this is not a packing list on what to pack, these are things you should have sorted before you leave on your working holiday to Australia.

1. Bank Account- Set up your Australian bank account before you leave you can do this online and then just collect your card once you arrive.
2. Make sure your passport has at least 6 months left on it from when you are planning to leave.
3. You will need a place booked/have somewhere to stay for the first few days when you arrive, and make sure you have the address of the place you are staying.
4. You know how to get from the Airport to where you are staying, are you getting a shuttle or public transport.
5. Take about $100 cash with you minimum for when you land. You never know what you might need it for and it's always good to have some local currency, just in case there is a problem with your bank for example.
6. You have transferred your money into your Australian bank account so it will be in there when you arrive All you need to then do is go and collect your card and you will then be able to access your money.
7. Obviously you will have some flights booked whether it's a one way ticket or a return. I would recommended getting a one way ticket as you never know where you might be flying home from, what if you decide to go to Asia, or a different part of the country.
8. Get some travel insurance bought, so it is valid from the day you leave Australia until the day you are planning on coming back.
9. Make sure that you have a visa and the confirmation all printed of so when you pass through customs on the other side you have proof if they ask for it. You usually wont be asked as it is done all electronically now,

but better safe than sorry.

10. I would also have a CV and cover letter wrote up before you depart and put them on a memory stick. Even print a couple out so you can start applying for jobs as soon as you arrive.
11. Immunisations, make sure you have been to the doctors and got all the necessary jabs. Tell them where you are planning on going and make sure you're all up to date.
12. If you have medication, make sure you have also asked your doctor about this and get all the medication you will need.
13. Take some spare passport photos, just in case as you never know when you might need them.
14. I would also have a document folder which you should keep in your hand luggage and just keep all the important documents in it such as; passport photocopy, visa copies, passport photos, any confirmations such as accommodation, bank information and print bank related emails, travel insurance, flight tickets etc.
15. Also apply for a tax file number so you can start getting paid sooner, this can be done online.
16. One that a lot of people forget but it is very important is make sure your phone is unlocked. When you get to Australia you're going to be getting a new sim card, so if your phone is unlocked you can then just stick your new sim straight in and away you go.
17. Also plan a few ways which you can keep in touch with family and friends, Skype, Facebook, email, whatsapp.

## Chapter 40-What To Pack

This is probably something that will be quite difficult for some people, especially if it is your first time travelling for such a long period, what on earth do you pack for a year away? I wouldn't worry about it too much as you can always buy stuff out there like if you forget shampoo or swimming trunks but below is a list of everything you might need. This was my packing list, so it is suited towards a guy, if your a girl you are probably going to want to add some more of your own things make up, bras, female hygiene products etc. This list has everything which I needed on it, you might want to take extra stuff, or you might want to leave some stuff off, but I found it had everything I needed personally on it, tailor it to suit you.

*(Packing for Australia)*

When travelling I would also take two bags my main backpack which would have the majority of things in and would go in hold luggage on planes and buses. You would probably be best with a backpack between 60-100 litres in size depending on how much stuff you want to take. I had an 80 litre rucksack. I would then have my hand luggage which would be a rucksack I would often wear this on my front when walking to and from bus station or to hostels or anywhere with all my luggage. I would use my hand luggage to keep all the most important items in and keep it with me at all times, so use it as hand luggage on the buses, planes. Then when getting to a hostel, I would empty this bag out and put all the important stuff such as passports, documents, money in the safety box which most hostels have in the rooms, failing that just in my pillow case. I would then use the rucksack for days out and trips to put food, water, my camera and any other stuff I would need in.

I also had a document folder, which I kept all my important documents in, including some spare money and my passport, I will also provide a list of stuff you might want to put in your document folder again you might not want to use it all. Using a document folder keeps everything safe and organised, so you know exactly where everything is should you need anything. It saves you panicking and having to search through all your bags, I just used to keep this in my rucksack.

Hand Luggage (Rucksack of some sort): Now the packing list for your hand luggage may look very long, but a lot of it is very small things that you can group together into different bags, such as electronics and wash stuff. Also remember in your hand luggage, you are allowed no liquids over 200ml, so buy the travel shower gels and deodorants and obviously no sharp or explosive items.

- Passport
- Hand tissues
- Debit card
- Student card
- 200 Australian dollars

- 20 GBP
- Earplugs
- Eye cover
- 2 pin adaptor for plane
- Notepad
- A pen
- Australian travel adapter
- Reading book
- Magazine
- Mobile phone
- Headphones
- Chargers for all your devices
- Camera and case
- Batteries (If your devices need them)
- Travel pillow
- Bum bag/money belt
- Paracetamol
- Sleeping pills (I did not end up using) only if required
- Imodium (for diarrhoea)- which you don't want on a +24 hour flight.
- Vaseline
- Hand sanitizer
- Moisturiser- your skin will get incredibly dry after being in the air for so long.
- Baby wipes/facial wipes- you can use these to wash your whole body.
- Playing cards
- Travel socks
- Spare t-shirt

- Spare underwear
- Spare socks
- Toothbrush and toothpaste
- Shower gel
- Deodorant
- Chewing gum
- Snacks: cereal bars, nuts, chocolate, sweets- as airport food alone probably wont suffice.
- Mints
- Water bottle
- Wallet
- Driving licence
- Small quick dry towel

Main Backpack: Again this is the packing list I used and it had everything I needed on it, you may want to add your own stuff or take stuff off, such as if you want to make your backpack lighter maybe take less clothing items. And girls will obviously want to take a few extra bits as mentioned previously.

- T-shirts × 5
- Socks × 8
- Underwear × 8
- Shirts × 3
- Board shorts × 2
- Jeans ×2
- Smart shorts × 2
- Hoodie
- Sweater

- Work/Business Shirt
- Tie
- Black trousers
- Trainers ×3 (Sports pair, and a couple daily pairs)
- Sandals/flip-flops/Crocs
- Walking boots
- Shoes
- Hats/Sun cap
- Jacket (Thin Coat as you wont need a big thick coat)
- Waterproof coat
- Sunglasses
- Belt
- Watch
- Pocket knife
- Towel
- First aid kit- plasters, antibacterial wipes, safety pins, band aid, paracetamol, ibuprofen, imodium, hay fever tablets, bite relief cream, condoms, cotton buds, antacid, burns cream, cough sweets.
- Cleaning/hygiene kit- in large unleakable wash bag; Toothbrush, toothpaste, shower gels, shampoos, deodorant, razor, shave gel, after shave, soap, tweezers, nail clippers, after sun ×2, sun lotion ×3, mosquito repellent, baby wipes.
- Toilet roll
- Bin liner
- Australian plug adapter
- Big combination loop padlock for lockers
- Batteries again if you're devices require them
- Sandwich box + knife fork spoon (For spare food, especially when

cooking in hostels)

Documents: These are the main documents you should take with you, most of them you will probably never need, but it's better to be safe than sorry and have it all should you need them.

- Passport photo copy
- Travel insurance photo copy
- CV photocopy
- Plane tickets and airline info photocopied
- Emergency contacts etc.
- Visa photocopy
- Driving licence photo copy paper version and photo ID card.
- Photocopies of all other Australia related e-mails that you've received.
- 4× passport photos
- Photocopy of bank statement showing sufficient funds
- Any photocopies of relevant qualifications
- Birth certificate photo copy
- Accommodation Emails Printed
- Vaccinations Record
- UK Bank Photocopies

## Chapter 41-Long Haul Flying

Long Haul flying can be horrible but it can also be a great time to relax and get away from the real world. I myself really enjoy flying, especially long haul as it gives you a chance to catch up on films, read books, do some writing and chat to other people on your flight, just generally relax and have no worries. The average flight from the UK to Australia is over 21 hours usually split in half by a stopover in another airport, most likely in Asia. Stopovers can be anywhere from just a couple of hours while the plane refuels, or an overnight layover of up to 15 hours or so. There are a number of things you can do to make your long haul flight to Australia more enjoyable.

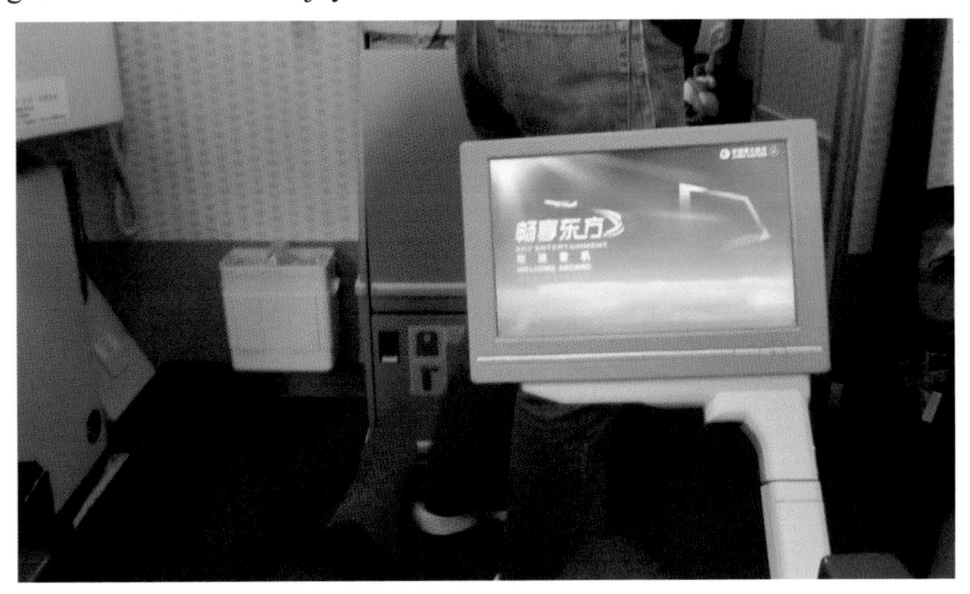

(In-flight entertainment, China Eastern)

What to do on your long haul flight?

- Watch a Film/Television- With nearly all long haul flights, in-flight entertainment is included, which is fantastic, how could you ever get bored with unlimited films, television shows and documentaries. With all the long haul flights I have been on, I haven’t even really needed my own technological entertainment in regards to television, as there is plenty to watch on the in-flight entertainment. There are also usually quite a few new films that would've been released in the last year which is perfect, a few hours can easily pass after a couple of films and a few episodes of television.

- Listen to Music- Just relax and listen to some music, before you go download the albums you've wanted to listen too for ages but have never had the time or just listen to the old stuff you really like.
- Read a Book- Take a book with you, lets be honest nobody wants to watch television for 12 hours straight everybody needs a break from that. Take a book to split it up, this can give your eyes a bit of a break. You could even take a puzzle book with crosswords or Sudoku to keep your brain active and stop yourself getting bored.
- Chat to Other Passengers- Chat to other passengers on your flight, chances are you are going to get sat next to to a range of people from all different backgrounds and cultures, get talking to them ask them where they're going, for how long what there plans are, where they're from, this can easily pass a few hours and who knows if you're lucky you might make a new friend in the country you're going too.
- Do some Writing- Whether it be professionally, a journal, a diary or whatever, dong a little writing can be fun, writing down maybe ideas, start writing that book you've always wanted to write, fill in your travel journal or maybe even start writing down or having a think about some business plans. Whatever it is, long flights are a great time to great creative and just think.
- Drawing- This one isn’t for me at all, but if you're arty and enjoying drawing then this is a great time to do some sketches of those ideas you have had but have never had time as you've been busy with routine life.
- Play Games/Cards- There is loads of technology out there with phones and tablets. You can easily download games, there are thousands of choices this also gives you a bit more interactivity rather than just watching television. Often there are also games on the in-flight entertainment, they are not very good, but still they make a change from television. I also like to travel with a pack of cards. These are great if you

meet someone on your flight and you get chatting why not play some cards with them, this can make time fly and can be a lot more fun than watching television or playing games.

- Sleep- Catch up on missed sleep and get ready for touchdown in the new country.

Things to pack in Hand Luggage: All of these are in the packing list above, but this is just a little bit more of an explanation as to why you might want these items in your hand luggage.

- Clean Pants, Socks and a T-shirt- To change into on your stopover, these will make you feel much fresher, particularly socks.
- Travel wash kit; Toothbrush, Toothpaste, Face wash, Deodorant, Baby Wipes.- This is a must when long haul flying after being on the plane for 12 hours your going to want to freshen up on your stopover before you land, use baby wipes to wash your body and armpits etc.
- Sleep Kit; Ear plugs, Eye mask and a blanket- This is a necessity if you want to get any sleep, they will help a lot and give you peace and quite if you need it. A blanket is not essential as they will usually have them in-flight if you need them but planes can get cold when they're in the air.
- Jumper- As said before planes can get cold when in the air, so don't just wear flip flops and a vest, because chances are you'll get cold.
- Book- To read.
- Headphones- Bring your own headphones, the headphones given in-flight are usually near enough useless, so bringing your own will give you a much more pleasurable experience, and particularly block out the background noise.
- 2 pin headphone adapter- This is an essential and a mistake a lot of people make when getting a flight. To be able to use your own headphones you need an adapter. As on a flight they need 2 pins, which

can be annoying if you forget it, you can pick them up of ebay for 99p.

- USB charger for all your electronics- Most long haul planes have USB ports where you can charge your phone so bring your charger.
- Flight and Travel Documents- Don't forget your flight and travel documents, if your phone goes dead or you can't access them it's best to have them all printed so you're prepared and don't miss any flights.
- Padlock- Not particularly needed, but if you have an overnight stopover, then this is good to be able to padlock your bag and helps to keep your belongings a bit safer.
- Passport- For obvious reasons.
- Wallet- With some money in a couple currencies, especially the country you are travelling too, student cards, driving license etc.
- Water Bottle- Rather than buy a water bottle after passing through security take an empty water bottle and ask one of the cafés in the departures lounge to fill it up for you.
- Some food- Take some food with you, even though you will get food on the plane chances are you are going to get hungry mid flight and plane food wont satisfy it. Take some snacks, not things like crisps as they take up a lot of room, stuff like chocolate, crackers, sweets, mints and chewing gum to freshen your breath. Take a wrap to for something more substantial. It's better to take a wrap than a roll or sandwich as these get crushed easily and take up lots of room.
- Camera- To take photos, this is not essential if you have a phone with a camera.
- Phone
- Tablet- If you have one for games and films, not essential though.
- Moisturiser- After being on a plane for 12 hours trust me your skin will thank you.
- Vaseline

With Layovers the best thing to do is to make the most of the open space have a walk around, go look in the shops, have a look in the electronics stores, book shops and all the other miscellaneous shops that are around. In airports there are also often places called rest rooms or sleep spots, particularly in the more established larger airports. If you know you have a long layover research online what the airport has to offer in regards to shops, sleeping areas and entertainment. Singapore airport has different entertainment zones for different types of television and also huge areas for sleeping. Some airlines also offer airport vouchers when you book a flight so you can buy some food. Also when flying long haul try to plan when you are going to sleep in reference with your flight and what time you land, to help cure the jet lag. This will make your first few days in Australia much more pleasurable. Many of the airports also have free Wifi, with some you can just connect straight up, but with others you will have to go to the information desk and ask for the free Wifi code and you can set it up yourself. Some airports even have computers you can use. As said before if you know you have a long layover, research the airport before so you know what's available to you.

## Chapter 42-Leaving Home

Finally Leaving home, it completely depends on the type of person you are as to how you will cope with this, I myself was so incredibly excited. I wasn't really thinking about leaving behind my friends or family to be honest. I just wanted to get on the plane and jet of to a new exotic country, meet new people and have some incredible experiences of my own.

But for some people leaving behind your family, friends, home and all the comforts associated with this might be difficult. Remember this isn't just a two week vacation, this is going to the other side of the world for a year, probably by yourself to start with too. But lets not forget with modern technology fast improving it's becoming easier and easier to keep in contact with people from all over the world. Once you get comfortable with the time difference that is, because in Australia the evening will be the UK's mornings, and Australia's mornings the evenings of the day before in the UK. There are loads of ways to keep in touch when away, Skype, what's app, Facebook, Emails and that just a few of the most popular ones, so keeping touch and letting everyone know what your up to as well as finding out what's going on back at home will be no problem at all.

Before leaving you will have a range of feelings and emotions going through you too, as it gets closer and closer to your flight. I myself was incredibly excited but also a little nervous which is going to be expected especially if your young and it's your first time away, but there is no need to worry, as long as you have all your main documents, like mentioned in the list above and have done a little bit of research it'll be a breeze. It does come up on you fast though that's for sure, I remember one minute I was in high school sat in a crappy classroom dreaming of the beautiful beaches of Australia and then before I knew it I was waving my parents goodbye. Do remember though it's not just an exciting day for you, but for your family also watching you fly off after having you around for 18 or so years it's also going to be nervy for them. Obviously if your a bit older and have been travelling before you're going to have experienced all this and will know what I'm talking about.

Another thing I would recommend to do before you leave home, particularity in the last weeks is make sure you spend some time with your family and friends before you leave. Go for your last night out with your mates, go out with your sister or brother for the day and spend some time with your parents. As excited as you will be to leave home, like I was, just wanting to get away into the bigger world, trust me in saying you'll appreciate those days out and trips you took when you do get to Australia.

Now these things may sound obvious but there are certain things I would recommend doing before you leave home they are not essential things like what were mentioned in the check list of stuff to do before you leave home, but you might want to do them:

- Get a haircut- you'll be far to busy enjoying yourself when you get to Australia to even think about getting a haircut.
- Confirm your flights and check in online if possible.
- Chuck away your old home country sim card and make sure the contract is cancelled so your not paying it.
- Make sure all other memberships in your home country are cancelled, such as gym memberships, magazines, online subscriptions, sports clubs etc.
- Make sure you leave some money in the bank for when you return home, I would recommend about £1000 if possible, because when you get home your going to want to get your phone re sorted, buy some winter clothes etc.
- Take a picture with your family before you leave?
- Leave important copies with people at home such as passport copies, visas and flight details.
- Make sure you have put all of your important home country stuff such as bank cards, loyalty cards and important documents you don't need to take with you into a draw on their own, so you know exactly where they are for when you get back.

## Chapter 43-Arriving Home

Now this might sound like a crazy and very depressing section, because you probably haven't even left for your new adventure to Australia yet, but unfortunately it is something which creates much discussion among frequent travellers, and how often people that don't travel for long periods will never understand. The culture shock of arriving home, after doing so many incredible things, meeting new people and you yourself as a person changing so much. Only to return home and for everything to be the same, nothing different at all, people in the same jobs, same houses and the same people walking through the streets. It's quite often called holiday blues which you have probably experienced, but after a year it's a whole different ball game.

You will probably to begin with find it very hard to adjust and get back into a normal working life, especially if you haven't worked for a while. Getting back into a job and a routine after just being free, and being able to do what you want, see the things you want to see and just leave if you got bored quite difficult. Some people even get quite depressed, me now still 8 months on since leaving Australia, still look back and think about the warm beaches and BBQs while I'm stuck inside my room in London studying, looking out the window when it's grey and miserable. You might also find that there is no-one you relate to any more back at home, as you have moved on and changed so much, that you just don't have the same views as a lot of people back home.

But that's the thing about travelling, when you do return home you shouldn't look at it in a negative way, look at it positively, start planning your next adventures. Go home to see all your family and friends, tell them about all your amazing adventures. I think in these situations you need to keep yourself motivated and have things planned for when you return home, set yourself some goals this will get you excited rather than down about coming home.

How to avoid post travel blues:

- Don't jump straight back into work as soon as you arrive home, take a week or two to catch up with friends, go on a few days out, relax and explore you home town again.
- Sort out all your photos, maybe make some sort of scrap book, write a journal, something which you can use to recall on you amazing adventures in a fun way.
- Make more adventures, instead of big trips like to the other side of the world, make weekend trips with your mates.
- Try doing some new things as said previously, set yourself some goals, maybe your going to university, or want to start saving and planning your next travels something to look forward and move towards.

These are just a couple things that might help you get back on your feet and into a normally daily routine which you soon will after the initial few weeks of being home.

As said before rather than being down about returning home, you should be excited for it, you can eat all that proper home cooked food again that you haven't tasted in months. You get your own room and space to actually be with yourself. You know your going to have a decent shower that actually works and is warm. You will have nothing to plan such as where your going next, or booking a room or getting to places you can just sit back and relax, you can watch television again.

Returning home is an inevitable part of any travel adventure, whether it's after a few months or a few years, it's essentially going to happen at some point but embrace it. Use it as something to look forward to for after your travels. But firstly…. ENJOY YOUR ADVENTURE and all the amazing memories your going to make, places your going to see, people your going to meet, exotic foods your going to be trying and new experiences your going to have.

Printed in Great Britain
by Amazon